MEDITATIONS ON HAPPINESS

I0089391

MANFRED F. R. KETS DE VRIES

First published 2002 by Vermillion
Second edition published 2007 by iUniverse
Third edition published 2017 by KDVI Press

Finsgate
5–7 Cranwood Street
London
United Kingdom
EC1V 9EE
www.kdvi.com

ISBN 978-0-9954948-2-4

A catalogue record for this book is available from the British Library.
A catalogue record for this book is available from the Library of Congress.

TO THE PERSONAE IN MY WILD
STRAWBERRY PATCH

|

WILL THE PYTHIA
CREATE ABHISAMAYA?

TABLE OF CONTENTS

PREFACE

---

*Perhaps they are not stars, but rather
openings in heaven where the love of our lost
ones pours through and shines down upon
us to let us know they are happy.*

INUIT PROVERB

*It is more fitting for a man to laugh
at life than to lament over it.*

SENECA

*Happiness is when what you think, what
you say, and what you do are in harmony.*

MAHATMA GANDHI

Almost two decades have passed since I wrote this essay on happiness. As with much of my writing, my reflections on the subject were a consequence of my personal experiences. As I have grown older, I have become even more aware of the temporary nature of happiness. Happiness can be compared to a sky filled with clouds. When the clouds open, we are enveloped by sunshine, which makes us happy. But the feeling is not going to last. Clouds are ever-present—and when they cover the sun, they make us feel low. But then, very often, the sun comes out again. This interchange of sun and clouds makes our life's journey an emotional roller coaster. Happiness is a transient and elusive experience. Our challenge is to recognize and make the best of happy moments when they come our way. And we should not give up or lose hope; happiness is always there somewhere, now and in the future.

I was not in the happiest of moods when I originally wrote this essay. Since then I have found solace in the verse from Ecclesiastes, "In much wisdom is much grief, and he that increases knowledge increases sorrow." Now, having passed my own "best before" date, the Chinese definition of happiness—having someone to love, something to do, and something to hope for—seems even more appropriate. When we are young, we feel immortal, but there comes a time when we begin to realize the tragic transience of things. As we grow older, we become increasingly aware that we would be wise to look for happiness in the small things of life. But to be able to do so, we have to look into ourselves. Happiness starts from within. We are often the authors of our own unhappiness. Far too often, we regress to thinking negatively and forget to count our blessings.

Being unhappy comes with a high price attached. This is borne out by many studies of happiness. For example, according to the World Health Organization, a large proportion of the world's population is very unhappy. Depression and other mental health problems are omnipresent. This situation begs for action, as happy people are healthier people, both mentally and physically. There are several reasons for this. Happy people cope more effectively with stress and trauma, they have more energy, and they are more resilient. They have a more robust immune system, so are less likely to get sick, increasing their potential longevity. They have better relationships with other people, have richer social networks, have more friends, and are more likely to have fulfilling marriages (including a lower divorce rate). From a leadership perspective, happy people are more productive and more creative. One conclusion we can draw from these studies is that happiness is not a luxury. Being happy or unhappy seriously affects the quality of our lives. This implies that we should take a proactive stand vis-à-vis the happiness equation.

It's risky to suggest a "prescription" that will increase the probability of happiness, as we all have own ideas of what makes us happy. However, I'm prepared to take the risk and suggest four essential components for a happiness remedy. But if it's to be effective, we have to start by accepting that we are responsible for creating our own happiness. Happiness is a matter of choice. It's an inside job. It doesn't come ready made; it's not dependent on position, power, prestige, or money. We have to make it happen.

The first is to build and maintain a supportive network of family members and friends. The quality of our relationships with other people is an essential ingredient of happiness. It is a good indicator when our family members are our friends, and our friends become family members. Second, we have to be able to manage envy. Out of the seven deadly sins, envy is the one that's no fun at all. Envy is an infectious disease. Suffering from envy is like dosing yourself with a slow-working poison. If we only count other people's blessings, but not our own, we are in trouble. We will only find happiness when we stop comparing ourselves to other people and learn to be satisfied with what we already have. Third, we must consciously practice forgiveness. Holding on to anger about things that have happened in the past is another form of self-poisoning. Forgiveness means making peace with our past. It is a source of strength, a gift to ourselves that sets us free. Although forgiving will not change the past, it lays the foundation for a better future. Without it, we can only look forward to an endless cycle of resentment and retaliation. The fourth component is gratitude. Counting our blessings and expressing gratitude to others improves our state of mind. One of the secrets of being happy is to make other people happy, because happiness depends far more on what we give than what we get.

Once, while I was in Washington, DC, I visited the Phillips Collection. Among the paintings on display was Pierre-Auguste Renoir's *Le déjeuner des canotiers* (The Luncheon of the Boating Party). This painting captures an idyllic afternoon as Renoir's friends share food, wine, and conversation, sitting on a balcony overlooking the Seine. It's clear that they enjoy each other's company, and that they are happy. I hope that all of us, at times, have experiences similar to what Renoir has caught here—a feeling of togetherness that we wish could last forever—and that the new edition of this essay will bring the reader some pleasure, including happiness.

1
INTRODUCTION

One is never as unhappy as one thinks,
or as happy as one hopes to be.
FRANÇOIS DE LÀ ROCHEFOUCAULD

Life is an onion.
You peel it off one layer at a time,
and sometimes you cry.
CARL SANDBURG

There is no cure for birth or death
except the capacity to enjoy the
interval.
GEORGE SANTAYANA

"Animals are happy as long as they have health and enough to eat," observed Bertrand Russell in his essay *The Conquest of Happiness*. "Human beings, one feels, ought to be, but in the modern world they are not, at least in a great majority of cases." People can be happy only when they feel "part of the stream of life," he observed, "not a hard separate entity like a billiard-ball which can have no relation with other such entities except that of collision." In other words, people need people. If we want to acquire happiness, looking in the mirror won't help; we need to look out the window.

Unfortunately, all too many people are like Russell's billiard-balls. Unable to reach out to others, they're islands onto themselves, self-focused and withdrawn; they're mirror-gazers rather than window-watchers. Eventually, through rampant individualism, they create a veritable prison for themselves, a self-imposed cage of unhappiness. Trapped in neurotic thoughts, they not only make themselves miserable, they also make other people miserable. And they don't know how to free themselves. What action they should take to become happy is beyond them; they haven't a clue how to be good to themselves.

The famous filmmaker Ingmar Bergman, in his film *Wild Strawberries*—an autobiographical tale in disguise—tells the story of an old man, Isak Borg, who embarks on two journeys, one from Stockholm to Lund to receive an honorary doctorate, the other into his inner world. To all outward appearances Isak Borg is a very successful man, a respected medical doctor and scientist. However, his personal life reveals a very different picture. His relationship with his aging mother is devoid of warmth, while that with his father (who is apparently out of the picture) is all but nonexistent; very little love is lost between Borg and his older brother; Borg's marriage, which was plagued by adultery and unhappiness, has ended in divorce; and Borg has a very distant relationship with the son of that marriage—his only offspring. Worse yet, the son is showing a relational pattern very like his own: an icy formality has crept between father and son. Given this relational morass, it is no surprise to learn, in the introduction to the film, that Borg's outlook on life has become, over time, increasingly "seen through a glass darkly." A sense of pessimism has crept upon him concerning the entire human race. Distraught at the way his life has turned out, he has withdrawn from most human interaction.

During the journey from Stockholm to Lund, Isak Borg—accompanied by his daughter-in-law (who plays a guiding role like that of Dante's Beatrice)—is confronted with various scenes from his past. Many of these scenes, which revolve around critical incidents, elicit unhappy memories. To counter the feelings these memories stir up—to avoid being overwhelmed by anxiety and misery—Borg makes an effort to recall incidents of happiness. He tries to return to his "patches of wild strawberries" (the phrase that's the title of the film in Swedish), symbols of the sweetness of life—memories of the fleeting moments of bliss and happiness that we all cling to. As the journey progresses (and Borg is influenced by a number of significant character-building experiences), his outlook on life begins to change. He becomes happier, more playful. He tries to reach out to people. Unfortunately, this transformation occurs when life's clock stands at a few minutes to midnight.

Reflecting on happiness tends to send a person on a trip down memory lane. Writing this commentary on happiness has taken me back to my own "patches of wild strawberries," but it's also returned me to the many thorn bushes I've encountered in my life's journey. There are echoes in my own background of both Bertrand Russell's essay and Ingmar Bergman's film. Not surprisingly, then, writing about happiness has been a conflicted process for me. While I've found great pleasure in both the aesthetic aspect of writing (the creation of something tangible) and the pragmatic aspect (the creation of something meaningful), that satisfaction has at times been overshadowed by the personal journey into the self that thinking about happiness inevitably triggers.

It's my hope that in these pages I can offer some guidance to readers in their search for happiness. Happiness is a hard topic to pin down, however. Feelings of distress are much easier to tackle than are the so-called positive feelings. They're much more definite,

more concrete. Though hard-nosed businesspeople may find it unfortunate, happiness isn't quoted on the stock exchange. It's not something to which a specific value can be attached. It's far less tangible than that—far too elusive. Happiness sneaks up on us, and it slips out of our hands just as quickly. It's often a totally unexpected gift. And yet slippery though happiness may be, its pursuit remains one of the major preoccupations of humankind. I'll try to shed some light on the topic by looking at it from various angles. My attitude is that it's better to have *some* clarity about this elusive subject than to abandon it altogether.

Although happiness is rarely mentioned as a goal on a résumé or a corporate report, the topic is nonetheless hard to escape professionally. Over the years, as a professor in Leadership Development and Human Resource Management, I've studied and given many lectures on the human life cycle, career development, leadership, organizational and personal change, and individual and organizational stress. I've listened to many presentations by executives agonizing over the vicissitudes of their careers. Furthermore, as a psychotherapist and psychoanalyst I've worked to help people make sense of their life's voyage; I've tried to be a guide in their internal and external journeys. And in each of these roles, over many years, I've seen the question of happiness pop up again and again as a key theme. People the world over, from the top-floor corner office to the assembly line, wonder, What can I do to become happier? What can I do to improve the quality of my life? What's gone wrong in my work and relationships? Are there ways I can "repair" the conflicts that I've created? Nothing triggers the imagination of an educator more than questions to which he has no cut-and-dried responses.

In the pages that follow, I first try to distill a general definition from the ether of our culture. Then, after a brief look at the research on happiness, I turn to a Chinese saying which states that the recipe for happiness is "someone to love, something to do, and something to hope for." I review each of these three dimensions, trying to shed light on the themes of love, work, and hope. This in turn leads me to an exploration of the need for balance and a look at the dichotomy between outward success and inner success. I also discuss the role of social comparisons and envy in the context of happiness, the important role of "play" in people's lives, and the relationship between stress and health. Finally, in the summing up, I address humankind's "exploratory" needs—our needs to strive for authenticity, to search for meaning, and to know ourselves. In the last section I make a few comments about the attainment of wisdom.

I've decided to take a somewhat different approach in presenting my ideas here. Instead of cluttering these pages with scientific references, I've kept my discourse relatively simple—an approach that may horrify my more scientifically inclined colleagues. The ideas presented in these pages are, for the most part, my personal meditations on happiness. Though my own observations are based on personal experience, that doesn't mean that they're of necessity idiosyncratic. On the contrary, they're based on years of immersion in relevant literature in the field, particularly in the areas of psychoanalysis, social psychology, developmental psychology, family systems theory, cognitive theory, and psychotherapy. For a number of reasons I've felt a growing need to write on this topic. But I suspected that if I were to tackle it in the traditional, academic way, my findings wouldn't touch readers in a manner that would help them increase their happiness quotient. So I've deliberately taken a more casual approach. I hope that readers will excuse me for putting the usual rigor aside. And although, as I said, my meditations on happiness haven't emerged in a vacuum, I take full responsibility for any idiosyncrasies that are included.

2
THE ELUSIVE CONCEPT OF HAPPINESS

|

And what is Life?—an hour glass on the run
A mist retreating from the morning sun
A busy bustling still repeated dream
Its length?—A moment's pause, a moment's thought
And happiness? A bubble on the stream
That in the act of seizing shrinks to naught.
JOHN CLARE ("WHAT IS LIFE?" THE ENGLISHMAN'S FIRE-SIDE)

Two happy days are seldom brothers.
BULGARIAN PROVERB

|

The French philosopher Jean de la Bruyère once said, "For man there are only three important events: birth, life, and death; but he is unaware of being born, he suffers when he dies, and he forgets to live." Obviously, de la Bruyère had a well-developed predisposition toward unhappiness. He didn't enjoy the intermission, shall we say. My objective here, unlike his, is to *concentrate* on the intermission in an effort to better understand what happiness is all about.

The desire for happiness is a universal human characteristic. It was so well developed in the ancient Greeks that they formulated a self-realization theory centered on happiness: *eudaimonism*. Literally, *eudaimonia* means "good spirit" (*eu* plus *daemon*), a word that's usually translated "happiness." In his *Nicomachean Ethics,* Aristotle examined a range of human experiences. According to him, the highest experience for humankind—and the only true passion—is the attainment of happiness. His definition of happiness is the state of the soul in accordance with virtue. Aristotle saw the search for personal well-being as the most important striving for humankind—the supreme goal of all human activity. *Eudaimonia* is attained, he said, by having a well-ordered lifestyle and engaging in those activities for which one is best suited. He realized that the attainment of happiness is never easy, however. To use his words, "One swallow does not make a summer, neither does one fine day; similarly, one day or brief time of happiness does not make a person entirely happy."

But the search for happiness didn't end with the Greeks. It has continued, unrelenting, through the centuries. Even in America's Declaration of Independence—a formal political document—we find the statement that it's humanity's inalienable "right to pursue happiness." Ironically, in spite of that reference, Thomas Jefferson (the document's primary author and a melancholic man) didn't know what the pursuit of happiness was all about. (And of course we realize that the *pursuit* of happiness is something quite different from its *attainment*.)

Many psychologists have tried to make the meaning of happiness more concrete by using words such as *self-actualization, peak experience, individuation, maturity, sense of flow,* and *subjective well-being.*

To most students of the topic these labels imply a sense that life as a whole is good, fulfilling, and meaningful. Unfortunately, *eudaimonia*—whatever label we assign it—appears to be only an ideal. Circumstance such as illness, injury, lack of education, lack of demand for the activity we want to take on, or inflexible government policies may prevent us from engaging in what would be best suited for us. And yet despite the ubiquity of such hindrances, for most of us today the pursuit of happiness is the ultimate goal of existence; it gives us hope and a reason for living, motivating us to go on in spite of life's hardships.

So why, despite that almost universal reverence for happiness, does it remain a mysterious concept? Why are we so cavalier about mentioning it but so clumsy in describing it? Is it because we haven't yet found the answer or because there *is* no answer? Some scholars who have written on happiness believe that it's one of those subjects that shouldn't even be explored. For example, the British writer Gilbert Chesterton noted, "Happiness is a mystery like religion, and should never be rationalized." He preferred not to probe any further, because he felt that the inquiry wouldn't lead anywhere. The American writer Nathaniel Hawthorn said, "Happiness is as a butterfly, which, when pursued, is always beyond our grasp, but which, if you will sit down quietly, may alight upon you."

But mystery or no mystery, sporadic efforts at deconstruction have been undertaken. For example, some people have argued that happiness isn't a place or a condition but a state of mind, something that comes from within us—a figment of the imagination, if you will. (That widely accepted view of happiness as a product of our inner world may have contributed to its cloaking in mystery.) Psychotherapists, on the other hand, have been known to compare happiness to the "Paradise lost" of early childhood—a vaguely remembered oceanic feeling of total togetherness with mother. They note that many of their patients have spoken of trying to recapture a fleeting memory of a mystical union they once knew—a memory that can be captured for a brief moment only. This perception has been institutionalized in the biblical story of humankind's fall from Paradise. It was Adam and

Eve's expulsion from the Garden of Eden that necessitated the quest for happiness.

Some psychiatrists and neurologists, however, have a more cynical outlook on the subject. They argue that happiness is nothing more than a physiological reaction, a product of body chemistry or the result of neurotransmitters set into motion. That viewpoint forces a debate over whether the happiness induced by drugs such as Prozac is real. If the emotion *feels* the same, derives from the same chemical source, is it *really* the same? Is that all there is to happiness? Should we leave it at that?

Regardless of the scientific approach they favor, most people who have thought about happiness don't see it as a long-term visitor; only occasionally, they say, does it make its home with us. And yet quite a few people, if asked, would say that they're basically happy— though sometimes more, sometimes less. Perhaps, then, we should compare happiness to the sun breaking through on a cloudy day. Though the rays are seen only sporadically, we know that the sun is always there. And if we try to chase the sun, we discover that it's moving away from us. Frustrating as this may be, it gives us something to strive for.

Ironically, the fact that happiness is never complete or constant is one of its virtues. A state of unbroken happiness would be monotonous at best, a nightmare at worst (like being in a state of perpetual orgasm). In fact, people who profess a constant state of happiness are likely to be diagnosed by psychiatrists as being hypomanic or in denial. In other words, there's such a thing as being *too* happy. Ups and downs are required to give our experiences color. Dark is needed to highlight light. As Dante Alighieri said in *The Divine Comedy (The Inferno)*, "No sorrow is deeper than the remembrance of happiness when in misery." Many of us have discovered that there's no pleasure without pain, just as there's no joy without sorrow. Carl Jung concurred when he noted, "Even a happy life cannot be without a measure of darkness, and the word *happy* would lose its meaning if it were not balanced by sadness. It is far better to take things as they come

along with patience and equanimity." Paradise without hell would be unimaginable. We need polarities; we need contrasts. There's a good reason Dante dwelled so long in the *Inferno* but moved relatively quickly through the *Paradiso*.

Having established that happiness is both elusive and ephemeral, what else can we say about it? What are its constituent components? We can't answer that question definitively, unfortunately, because happiness means different things to different people. It's a very subjective experience; we all have our own fantasies about what happiness is (or should be). Some people use the label *happiness* to describe a state in which they're no longer plagued by desire (even though not every past wish has yet been fulfilled). Others refer to happiness as the feelings attached to special moments retained in memory—a smile from a loving parent, a successful moment at school, a first love affair, the birth of a child, a reunion of the family, or a get-together with friends. Those of a scientific bent describe happiness as a sense of satisfaction with life as a whole, the absence of negative emotions or psychological distress, a sense of purpose in life, and feelings of personal growth. In all these definitions, though, a positive state of mind is key.

Despite the subjective nature of happiness, scholars of "positive psychology" or "subjective well-being" break happiness down into a number of component parts or mood states. They list among the more positive moods and emotions feeling states such as joy, elation, contentment, pride, affection, happiness, and ecstasy; among those feelings that counter happiness are guilt, shame, sadness, anxiety, fear, contempt, anger, stress, depression, and envy.

3
THE HAPPINESS EQUATION

There are three kinds of lies:
lies, damned lies, and statistics.
MARK TWAIN

That action is best, which procures the
greatest happiness for the greatest numbers.
FRANCIS HUTCHESON

If you can't convince them, confuse them.
HARRY TRUMAN

Issues of definition aside, most of us agree that obtaining happiness isn't an easy task. Like the Garden of Eden, it remains frustratingly out of reach. When I ask people if they're happy, I often get evasive and conflicting responses. Many, though, describe their lives as distinctly *un*happy. Philosophers, rarely the cheerleaders of the world, have elaborated on the matter. For example, Henry Thoreau believed that "most men live lives of quiet desperation," while Jean de la Bruyère claimed that "most men spend the best part of their lives in making their remaining years unhappy." The lexicographer Samuel Johnson was no optimist either, remarking that "human life is everywhere a state in which much is to be endured, and little to be enjoyed." The psychiatrist Thomas Szasz was even gloomier, alleging that "happiness is an imaginary condition, formerly attributed by the living to the dead, now usually attributed by adults to children, and by children to adults." The filmmaker and writer Woody Allen dressed his dark outlook in the light colors of tongue-in-cheek levity: "More than any other time in history, mankind faces a crossroads. One path leads to despair and utter hopelessness. The other, to total extinction. Let us pray we have the wisdom to choose correctly."

Are essayists, artists, and psychiatrists correct in making these gloomy statements? Or do their words reflect the dark *Weltanschauung* of only a selected few? Do people in these professions, given their concern for the transience of things, by nature have a more depressive outlook toward life? Perhaps so. Survey studies concerned with happiness result in optimistic numbers that are hard to ignore. On surveys of subjective well-being (conducted in many different countries and subcultures), *most respondents score themselves well above the neutral point on a scale of life satisfaction*. In other words, they generally score themselves as being more happy than unhappy.

Of course, we can always question the results of such studies, since they're based on self-reports. Many processes, unconscious as well as conscious, are at work when people engage in self-reporting, causing biased responses. For example, the "social desirability factor"—the human urge to be accepted by peers—might lead someone

23

to exaggerate happiness to maintain social acceptability. It's fair, then, to wonder whether people really *are* happy when they *say* that they're happy. Researchers who have tried to tackle that question have generally found convergent validation of self-reported happiness through surveys of family members and close friends. In my own questionnaire studies of mood states, however, I've found that a high percentage of people are quite talented at misleading those who are close to them (both at work and at home).

Reservations about self-reporting aside, why are the results so rosy? Why do people choose happiness over unhappiness, even when life is hard on them? At the most basic level, perhaps it's a survival mechanism. If we want to survive as a species, we need to avoid the withdrawal and apathy that negative mood states engender. Brooding and navel-gazing don't make for effective action; on the contrary, they impede our efforts to look after ourselves, provide for our family, and serve our community. Because we're social animals, the networks we build are important to building and maintaining society. Our human world functions best when people are able to reach out and engage with others in social interaction. Man alone is much more vulnerable than man as a group. Given all the adversities that we encounter, a team, a group, a clan, a tribe, a nation has much greater efficacy than an individual alone.

When I was in the rain forest of Central Africa hunting with the pygmies, who are a relatively primitive tribe, it became clear to me that their success as a people was very much influenced by their positive outlook toward life. The pygmies were dependent on each other for survival. They hunted together; they gathered roots and fruits together; they built shelters together; they took care of each other's children. All these activities were done to the accompaniment of cheerful banter— the fruit of a constructive, optimistic outlook on life. From my observations, pygmies tend to be happy people. They have a knack for reframing experiences in a positive way, and they love to laugh and sing. Jokes and laughter were common methods of resolving problems between members of our hunting team. The pygmies' willingness to express positive emotions (and their outright enjoyment of those emotions) makes conflict resolution much easier in all phases of pygmy life. In fact, I discovered quite quickly that a silent pygmy camp—a camp without expressed happiness—is a camp that has problems.

Some social psychologists use the label "the Pollyanna Principle" (named after the heroine of a children's book who always had a sunny disposition) to describe the tendency of humankind to process pleasant information more efficiently than unpleasant. The French expression *la vie en rose* (which in English equates with seeing things through rose-coloured glasses) also describes this particular behavior pattern. All too often, when in my initial interviews with people I ask them about their past, they tend to portray a rather idyllic picture. This picture is quickly shattered, however, when I probe somewhat deeper and begin to see reality. As a matter of fact, cynics might say that nothing is more responsible for the "good old days" than a bad memory.

Interestingly enough, according to evidence coming from studies done with identical twins, the state of subjective well-being that we call *happiness* appears to be partially heritable. In other words, there seems to be a genetic component to the ability to be happy, although estimates for the size of the influence vary widely (with the highest estimates coming in at about fifty percent). Whatever the true percentage may be, current thinking is that genetically based personality dispositions (traits and temperament) predispose people to be more or less happy. This heritability factor may explain why for many people the baseline for happiness remains relatively stable during the lifespan (with variations occurring on a day-to-day or even an hour-to-hour basis). The temperament bestowed on us at birth seems to play a significant role in the happiness equation.

The French author François de la Rochefoucauld reached the same conclusion without the benefit of scientific research: "Happiness and misery depend as much on temperament as on fortune." Does this mean that we might as well give up trying to improve our feeling states? Fortunately not! Life is not that deterministic. Because there's no specific gene for happiness, genetics is only part of the picture. While we may be genetically hard-wired with certain traits, this wiring in our brains isn't a static, final condition. Developmental experiences and current life events make a significant difference to our state of mind. Our interpretation of life circumstances (subtly influenced by biological factors) has a major effect on our feelings of happiness. Most scholars who have researched this topic (geneticists included) agree that life circumstances have an influence on subjective well-being. A large measure of what determines the way we feel, think, behave, and act is a result of our upbringing and social and cultural forces. In other words, while genetics plays a part, happiness and unhappiness are also *learned behaviors*. Many contextual factors play a role in whether we are happy or not.

In addition to showing that people have a tendency toward happiness, survey studies confirm that money doesn't bring happiness. Rich people aren't necessarily happier than people with more modest means, and we don't need to be wealthy and/or famous to be happy. That said, however, I should add that happiness is independent of income level only for those whose basic needs have been met. Among the poorly fed and provided for, there seems to be a positive correlation between income and happiness. The slight increase in happiness that we see when income rises at the lower end of the income range levels off, however, at the higher levels. At *all* levels, what seems to matter more than *absolute* wealth is the person's *perceived* wealth. Feeling rich requires having desires that we can afford. All of us are wealthy to the extent that, rather than seeking to *have what we want,* we seek to *want what we have.*

Furthermore, happiness has a slight positive correlation with social status and level of education, perhaps because these factors often raise income levels (thereby making people at the higher level of the income curve less preoccupied by financial concerns). Job status/satisfaction has an even stronger positive correlation with happiness. People of working age with no job at all are unhappier than people who are employed. Numerous studies have shown that unemployment contributes to an array of psychological disorders ranging from apathy and irritability to various somatic stress symptoms. These studies also suggest, however, that retired people on the average are happier than people who are still working (although retired people who held interesting jobs that provided a great deal of job satisfaction miss the challenge of their previous activities).

Whether we are young or old doesn't make a difference in the happiness equation. Self-reports of happiness, taken on average, favor no particular age. However, childhood happiness by no means guaranties happiness later on, and vice versa, despite the genetic component. Our opening reference to Bertrand Russell's experience is indicative. Russell seems to have become happier as life went on. Some happy children turn out to be quite neurotic and unhappy as adults, while many people whose childhood was quite unhappy turn out to be happier as life progresses. Furthermore, age can change the intensity of happiness. When we get older we aren't necessarily less happy, but our feelings tend to mellow; we tend to have fewer high highs and low lows—in other words, our average feeling of happiness become more stable.

Happiness is as oblivious to gender as it is to age; it doesn't matter whether we're male or female. As with age, the peaks and valleys of happiness between genders may be somewhat different—women are more likely to experience greater ups and downs in positive and negative feelings and moods—but the average level of happiness is about the same. Men and women are different, however, in experiencing certain forms of unhappiness. For example, women are twice as likely as men to suffer from depression, while men are more likely to act in antisocial ways or become alcoholic.

People seem to have a remarkable "elasticity" as far as happiness is concerned. Social science research points out that we adapt to new situations very quickly. Objective life circumstances play a temporary role in mood states, but they have little effect in the long term. Extreme peaks and valleys in happiness or unhappiness are quickly neutralized through a process of habituation and we return to our customary state of being.

This human tendency may need some further explanation. Let's look at an example. When I'm at my house in the South of France in the summer and eating white peaches on a daily basis, this activity doesn't bring me the same level of temporary pleasure that miraculously finding a peach in my backpack while hiking in the mountains of the Pamirs would. I've often "hallucinated" about these peaches when on top of a mountain, exhausted and dehydrated. But that pleasure I anticipate lessens with continuous satisfaction.

The predecessors of modern economics knew this phenomenon quite well when they introduced marginal utility theory. The father of marginal utility theory, Herman Gossen, expressed this phenomenon in his "first law" by explaining that the first strawberry one puts in his mouth is much more satisfactory than the ones that follow. We all know from our own experience that this is true: as we eat more and more strawberries, we eventually get satiated, and we don't experience the same level of satisfaction as we continue eating. What was once a high, memorable experience, quietly slips away. New stimuli need to be pursued to arrive at similar feelings. Fortunately, some experiences—among them, eating strawberries, having a good meal, and having sex—become exciting again after some time has passed. Apparently, desire resuscitates itself.

This human tendency to quickly adapt to a new state of being, reverting to our customary emotional baseline, is called "hedonic equilibrium." Some social scientists use the more negative label "hedonic *treadmill*," suggesting that we adapt to changing circumstances to the point of emotional neutrality. Initial highs eventually give way to complete indifference. As an example, million-dollar lottery winners—after a temporary state of euphoria—very quickly bounce back to their ordinary, more pedestrian mood state of moment-to-moment happiness. Whatever the happiness trigger, personality predispositions such as temperament may play an important role in bringing people back to their original equilibrium.

Since we can be satiated by happiness, one might ask how long a person could really be happy in heaven. While theologians usually describe hell in great detail, they have very little to say about heaven. Perhaps that's because descriptions of life in heaven make it sound rather tedious—happiness, happiness, and more happiness. None of the activities that are really exciting—but sinful, of course—take place in heaven.

Although some of us may find it difficult to imagine, even people who experience an extreme stroke of ill-fortune (a crippling accident, for example, or exposure to a life-threatening event such as cancer) can find happiness. The biblical story of Job is a signifier of that possibility. Although hardships aplenty came Job's way, he never doubted that there would be a time for renewed happiness. Studies have shown that people who have been in extremely stressful situations tend to be much less unhappy than others make them out to be. Many victims of extreme ill-fortune feel actually embarrassed for not being unhappier than outsiders think they should be.

Many people are able to reconstitute their lives and find new happiness after serious physical setbacks. The former movie star Christopher Reeve (well known for his role as Superman) is probably one of the better examples of such a turnaround in outlook. Despite an accident that paralyzed him, he has managed to overcome his depression about his condition and has found new meaning—and happiness—in life by becoming a spokesman for paraplegics.

Survey research suggests that the happier people are those who are married, don't belong to an ethnic minority group, have a positive self-esteem, are extraverted, and have a feeling of personal control.

Religion also contributes to happiness. Feeling close to God and believing in an afterlife help to give meaning to daily life, thereby creating a positive outlook. In addition, religion positively influences mental health in a more general sense. Because religion offers a kind of collective identity (through participatory experiences such as prayer and worship) and helps create social networks (through church, synagogue, mosque, temple, or other forms of membership), religious people have the benefit of social support. This plays a particularly important role in times of crisis.

People who engage in leisure activities, particularly sports and exercise, also seem to be happier. Leisure activities done in a group setting, such as participation in social clubs, choirs, or team activities, are often mentioned as sources of happiness. For people who are extraverted and optimistic, reaching out to others reinforces a positive state of mind. Holidays can also be a source of happiness, because they break the daily routine and reverberate with humankind's exploratory needs.

Furthermore, the more happier people among us refrain from dwelling excessively on the negative side of things (they are more optimistic), live in economically developed societies (implying societies with a stable political system and political freedom), have social confidants, and possess the resources to strive toward valued goals.

The question of causality looms large as we read these statistics. What contributes to (or is related to) what? What is the direction of causality? For example, are happiness and marriage correlated because marriage brings happiness or because happy people are more likely to find marriage partners? How does the interchange work? Is it the external events that make the difference, or is it our outlook on life—our *Weltanschauung?* Do people who find themselves in a perpetual state of unhappiness perceive and interpret the situations they're in more darkly than others do? The findings about happiness and self-esteem, extraversion, personal control, and optimism all point in this direction. Happiness may be, before everything, a state of mind—the way we look at the world. In other words, the way we think about the causes of our successes and failures in life really makes a difference.

4

OUR

WELTANSCHAUUNG

There is only one way to happiness and that
is to cease worrying about things which
are beyond the power of our will.
EPICTETUS

Every man is an architect of his own fate.
APPIUS CAECUS

Happiness does not depend on outward things,
but on the way we see them.
LEO TOLSTOY

A wit once said, "He fell in love with himself at first sight, a passion to which he has always remained faithful." Funny as this observation may be, narcissism is serious business. The satisfaction that narcissism brings is very transient, because self-centeredness hinders the outward focus that is essential to good relationships. Bertrand Russell noted that we should "aim at avoiding self-centered passions and at acquiring those affections and those interests which will prevent our thoughts from dwelling perpetually on ourselves. It is not the nature of most men to be happy in a prison, and the passions which shut us up in ourselves constitute one of the worst of prisons." Among the "passions" that can make us unhappy he listed fear, envy, competitiveness, the sense of sin, self-pity, and self-admiration. He concurred with the idea that, first and foremost, happiness is a state of mind. He had a point when he argued that extreme self-centeredness is a delusionary way of finding happiness. We have to evict the ghosts that plague us. The art of happiness is to neutralize or minimize the internal forces that torture us. We need to break out of our self-imposed prison. As the saying goes, "Smile and the world smiles with you." Happiness is like a magic potion we cannot pour on others without getting a few drops on ourselves.

Not only do we imprison ourselves with our self-centeredness; all too frequently we also take on the role of torturer (though admittedly one among many). We are our own worst enemy in searching out ingenious ways to make our lives miserable. But why do we do that if, as research findings suggest, happiness is largely dependent on our cognitive state—on how we interpret and respond to situations? Where do our ghosts come from?

In almost all cases we are prisoners of our past. As the Danish philosopher Søren Kierkegaard once said, "The tragedy of life is that you can only understand it backwards, but you have to live it forwards." Our internal theater—the themes that influence our behavior—is very much influenced by the kind of parenting we were exposed to. We internalize and model ourselves after the behavior of the people who took care of us during our impressionable years.

Developmental psychologists and cognitive theorists have demonstrated that much of our behavior is learned. The proof of the pudding is that all too often, when we unmask our torturer, we see familiar faces behind our own—the faces of the people who raised us. Their admonitions still haunt us: *Don't do that! Put on your jacket; you'll get sick if you don't! If you behave like that, you'll become like your uncle, and you know what happened to him! Don't listen to what your friend says—his parents are no good! Your grandmother was a saint, but your grandfather was a good-for-nothing—and you're behaving just like him! Don't play with that girl; she's a troublemaker!* Messages like these are internalized when we're young (since we model our behavior on that of our parents), and they have an effect on how we interpret life-events over the course of the years.

Many of us turn out to be proxies of our parents, sent on "missions impossible." We carry their ghosts with us in the form of feelings of shame, guilt, anger, anxiety, fear, and sadness. These internalized feelings may continue to haunt us later in life, the critical voices of our caretakers still echoing in our heads and influencing our outlook on life.

As an English proverb says, "All happiness is in the mind." The outlook that we carry into adulthood holds the key to our happiness, since events and situations can be interpreted in quite different ways. One person may see as positive the very challenge that another sees as negative. Let's look now at several ways in which outlook and happiness are related.

Internal Versus External Locus of Control

Psychologists sometimes distinguish between two ways of looking at the world. They categorize people as being either *internals* or *externals*, depending on their action orientation. An extreme internal is someone who thinks that he or she can do anything; nothing is impossible. Such people imagine that they are in control of their lives. Internals attribute events to themselves; they consider themselves master of their own destiny. They tend to be proactive and entrepreneurial. In contrast, extreme externals see themselves as being victimized by the environment; everything that happens is a question of chance or fate. Externals give up before they even start; they don't think that they can accomplish anything. More reactive than proactive, they lack a sense of personal efficacy. And yet giving up is the ultimate tragedy, because a defeatist outlook results in total passivity—a road that bypasses happiness.

In laboratory experiments in which dogs or rats were given electric shocks, those animals that had no way to avoid being shocked eventually suffered from paralysis of the will and become apathetic. In short, they gave up. Even in new situations they wouldn't try to help themselves. This belief that they couldn't make a difference is known as *learned helplessness*, as described by psychologist Martin Seligman. Like these research animals, human beings in extreme situations—a concentration camp, for example—often lose hope. Their experience teaches them that nothing they do makes a difference. These animal experiments suggest that our cognitive, learned outlook matters.

I've seen many situations of learned helplessness in organizations. For example, take the case of a company that for many years had been led by a conservative, autocratic leader. This person favored centralized power and took care of most of the decision-making. No initiative was permitted without his explicit permission; every decision had to pass through him. Eventually, this firm was acquired by a global company that had a very different outlook on business. When the new executives took the helm, they tried to disseminate their particular philosophy to the employees of the company through words such as *empowerment, entrepreneurship,* and *accountability.* But in spite of their encouragement to do things differently—to introduce more contemporary management practices—nothing happened. The employees continued in their usual ways, foregoing initiative and deferring to their supervisors on all decisions. Notwithstanding the new circumstances they found themselves in, the employees were frozen in dependency mode. They didn't know how to take a fresh look at managing the business. Some employees were so bewildered by the new corporate expectations that they left the company. Others, because of their lack of effectiveness, were asked to leave. Serious morale problems followed.

This period of confusion lasted for some time. Gradually, however, with the help of a number of newcomers, most of the remaining employees were able to transform their outlook. They discovered that making decisions on their own didn't carry a penalty—the new leadership had been serious when they said that employees were empowered to take action. They discovered that people who stuck their neck out and engaged in entrepreneurial activities were rewarded rather than punished—even when their experiments were less than successful. It took some time, however, for the employees' trained incapacity to disappear. The previous CEO had given the old employees too many "electric shocks" to allow them to believe that they had some control over their lives. Like the dogs and the rats in the research lab, the employees were initially incapable of moving forward.

The moral we can draw from such experiences is this: if we want a shot at happiness, we need to be proactive. Emulating internals, we need to believe that we can make a difference. When someone else writes the script—which is how life is in the externals' world—we're not really living, but just playing a part. Sitting down and waiting for miracles won't get us anywhere, while articulating and doing what we want in life may well lead to meaning and fulfillment. We need to follow our convictions. We need to tell ourselves that we're not merely creatures of circumstances; we're free agents.

It's clear that our *Weltanschauung* matters in the happiness equation. If we depend on others to make us happy, we will be endlessly disappointed. We have to take the initiative ourselves. Self-pity doesn't bring happiness, nor does quitting. Most people are as happy as they tell themselves to be. It's the way we think about our successes and failures that makes a difference. Do we dwell on our incapacity to do things? Do we blame others for our failure to solve problems? Or do we tell ourselves that *we can make a difference?*

Thus internals, who tend to have a more positive, active outlook on life, are more likely to experience moments of happiness than are externals. Perceived control—and even the *illusion* of control—usually has a positive effect on personal well-being and serves as a buffer against stress. Perceived loss of control or learned helplessness—the perception that all our actions will be futile—leads to a sense of hopelessness and is widely seen as a recipe for depression and other psychiatric disorders.

Optimism Versus Pessimism

The linkage between happiness and personality dispositions is evidenced in our level of optimism as well. Do we see the glass as half full or half empty? Are we optimists or pessimists? Optimists argue that we live in the best of all worlds, while pessimists *worry* that they are not. Optimists look at the bright side of things, seeing each defeat as a temporary setback. When faced with a bad situation, they perceive it as a challenge and work hard to turn it around. They have hope for a better future and believe that they can succeed in what they set out to do. Furthermore, they perceive others as having a positive view of them.

Such an attitude toward life makes optimists by definition happier than pessimists. And that optimism bears fruit: people who think positively are more likely to have positive things happen to them, they cope more successfully with stressful events, they enjoy better health (being less vulnerable to illness), and they're more successful. What's more, their optimism is contagious. One person's positive thoughts trigger positive thoughts in others.

In contrast, pessimists disqualify the positive—they see everything through a negative filter. Regrettably, that pessimism often becomes a self-fulfilling prophecy. Compounding the negative effects, pessimists may turn others off with their negative attitude, reinforcing their negative state of mind. While optimists create their own heaven, and enjoy the ride, pessimists are the architects of their own hell, taking on the role of torturer. Believing that bad events are inevitable and lasting, they give up hope easily. They experience a lack of efficacy to change the course of events in their lives.

Of course, any outlook toward life needs balance. Too much optimism—yes, there is such a thing!—leads to self-delusion and self-defeating action, while excessive pessimism leads to paralysis. If we are to engage in effective decision-making, we need the ability to distinguish between the things we can control and those we cannot—a distinction that healthy optimism heightens.

If we lack that ability—if we're externals with a pessimistic orientation—we have a susceptibility to cognitive distortions. As we saw earlier, those distortions are generally learned; they're holdovers from injunctions by our caretakers given at a vulnerable age. Examples of cognitive distortions are patterns such as all-or-nothing thinking (the tendency to see everything in black or white), magnification or minimization of specific situations (either exaggerating or diminishing certain events), jumping to conclusions (making an interpretation of an event without supporting evidence), and "labeling" (the inclination to put people into specific "slots").

When I deal with pessimistic people in my psychoanalytic practice, I try to help them reframe the way they look at life and at specific situations, encouraging them to take small steps to bring about change even when events seem out of their control. I encourage them to look at setbacks as challenges and to try harder rather than giving up. It's my belief—a belief supported by evidence—that we can *think* our way to success and happiness, just as we can think our way to failure and despair. Optimism is the best antidote to helplessness, enabling us to bounce back from defeat.

Extraversion Versus Introversion

Along with optimism and an internal locus of control, extraversion plays a role in happiness. Extraverts tend to be more sensitive to the external environment than are introverts. Because they react more strongly and more affirmatively to positive emotions in that environment, they seem to find it almost easy to be happy.

An indirect mechanism further links extraversion and happiness. Extraverts are better able than introverts to search out people and positively engage with them. Given societal demands for social involvement, this trait allows extraverts a better fit in the world. And because outgoing personalities feel more comfortable in social situations, they engage in *more* social activities. This explains why, in general, sociable, outgoing people have a greater sense of satisfaction with life. As the writer Aldous Huxley once said, "Happiness is not achieved by conscious pursuit of happiness; it is generally the by-product of other activities."

High Versus Low Self-Esteem

Another element of our *Weltanschauung* is our sense of self-esteem. For happiness to visit us we need a positive self-regard characterized by such qualities as self-acceptance and self-respect. Indeed, one of the best indicators of happiness appears to be how comfortable we are with ourselves. People who like themselves find it easier to open up to others rather than keeping their cards close to the chest. That self-disclosure, and the two-way communication that generally results, helps in creating bonds with others. People who engage in open communication have a wider social network, have more social support, and engage more in gratifying social undertakings.

People with low self-esteem, on the other hand, are more likely to indulge in socially withdrawn, self-centered, antagonistic, or brooding behavior. While those with high self-esteem see themselves as masters of their domain, believing that they can make a difference, those with low self-esteem tend to engage in scapegoating and other defensive behavior patterns. Furthermore, there is a strong correlation between low self-esteem and psychological disorders, especially depression.

This review of personality characteristics favorable to happiness brings us back to the question of nature versus nurture. Are positive self-esteem, extraversion, optimism, and an internal locus of control largely the result of genetic predisposition—that is, entirely predetermined—or do we have the power to affect our destiny? Fortunately, as we saw earlier, the genetic influence on personality traits isn't completely hard-wired. We're left with quite a bit of room to maneuver. We should view the personality dispositions we display in adulthood as an intricate interplay between nature and nurture. While the nature component is strong, there is ample space for developmental influences. We *do* have the power to affect our destiny, but we need to *want* to do that. We need to take a proactive stance.

5
DECONSTRUCTING
HAPPINESS

|

Not in Utopia—subterranean fields,—
Or some secreted island, Heaven knows where!
But in the very world, which is the world
Of all of us,—the place where, in the end
We find our happiness, or not at all!
WILLIAM WORDSWORTH

Enjoy yourself; it is later than you think.
CHINESE PROVERB

Life is a Cabaret, old chum
Come to the Cabaret.
FRED EBB

In an old Chinese saying, happiness is defined as consisting of three things: someone to love, something to do, and something to hope for. There's a lot of truth in this observation. We need love and hope in our lives, and we need activity. Sigmund Freud took a parallel tack, pointing out that the pillars of mental health are the ability to love and the ability to work. Unfortunately, workaholic that he was, Freud forgot to mention the play element that's an essential part of human nature. We all have an exploratory, motivational side—one that we see in small children as they experiment and try new things. Thus people who do work that feels like play are fortunate indeed.

Let's take a closer look at the three elements of that Chinese proverb: someone to love, something to do, and something to hope for.

Someone to Love

All of us need someone to love, someone we can feel close to and confide in. The first "love relationship" we experience (if we're among the lucky ones) is with our parents. Later, other family members come into the picture: grandparents, brothers and sisters, aunts and uncles, cousins. When we grow older, there are friends and perhaps a spouse and children. Sharing experiences with these people is part and parcel of the happiness equation.

Happiness cries out to be shared. It's like an embrace: only by sharing it is it possible to get enjoyment. In fact, happiness that's shared is double happiness, while happiness hoarded is empty. The secret of happiness is the ability to find joy in another's joy, the desire to make *other* people happy. To experience true happiness, we need to learn to forget ourselves, because self-centeredness and happiness are mutually exclusive. We need instead to be generative; we need to care about others. Many of us have seen this phenomenon in action: when we bring sunshine into the lives of others, we get some rays in return. Even the littlest things can produce moments of happiness—a smile, a hug, a heartfelt thank-you.

These little gestures can turn into glorious feelings for both giver and recipient.

The reason true happiness comes only through sharing is that the human need for connectedness runs deep. From birth onward, there are many fibers that connect us to the human community. As mentioned before, social networks are critical to a person's well-being. Attachment behavior is a deeply ingrained motivational need of humankind. Social scientists have gone to great lengths to describe this major need. The English psychiatrist John Bowlby has pointedly illustrated the vicissitudes of attachment behavior studying mother-infant interaction. Human beings have a great propensity for establishing affectional bonds with their mother and other caretakers as a step in establishing a feeling of security. Many forms of stress and disturbances such as anxiety, anger, and depression are the results of unwilling separations and loss.

Among humans there exists an innately unfolding experience of human relatedness. Humankind's essential humanness is found in seeking relationships with other people, in being part of something. No person can last as an island onto him- or herself—the literary fantasy of Robinson Crusoe notwithstanding. The need for attachment concerns the process of engagement with another human being, the universal experience of wanting to be close to others. It also concerns the pleasure of sharing and affirmation. When this need for intimate engagement is extrapolated to groups, the desire to enjoy intimacy can be described as a need for *affiliation*. Both attachment and affiliation serve an emotional balancing role by confirming the individual's self-worth and contributing to his or her sense of self-esteem. Having close ties to friends and loved ones and being a member of a community of people are essential aspects of becoming a person. They're critical not only to mental health but also to happiness.

Remember, though, that loneliness is not the same as being alone. *Being* alone is solitude; *feeling* alone is loneliness. The latter is an indicator of poverty of self. It signals an inability to reach out, to transcend one's personal sphere, and it suggests underdeveloped social skills. Worse yet, loneliness is self-perpetuating: people unable to reach out to others have little hope of breaking their loneliness pattern. And yet a Moorish proverb suggests that, "to die with others is better than living alone."

One of the most intense love experiences people have comes through close partnership. The most satisfying relationships people are involved in are the truly intimate ones. A relationship such as marriage brings out extremely intense feelings—including happiness. For many people, the intimacy of a true love affair results in many happy memories—memories that reinvigorate during down times. When a partnership works, this love between two people transcends sexuality, incorporating mutual attachment and true friendship.

Researchers on family dynamics have shown that the amount of time couples spend together—their level of companionship—determines marital as well as overall happiness. As Friedrich Nietzsche once said, "The best friend is likely to acquire the best wife, because a good marriage is based on the talent of friendship." When we experience genuine physical *and* psychological intimacy, we go from strength to strength. This intense relationship helps us to develop and grow; it serves as a base for both greater self-understanding and greater understanding of others. Bearing and raising children is often part of this learning process. Children are important as engineers of happiness because they're catalysts, helping their parents transform from a self-centered view to a more mature, exocentric perspective on life; in other words, they "teach" that happiness is often greater when it comes through giving rather than receiving. Thus, having children is a developmental experience that contributes to happiness.

Although the good memories that grow out of an enduring partnership serve as a buffer against the stresses of life, spouses can also play an important containment function, helping each other overcome conflict and anxiety. If there's mutual affection and trust in a marriage, the spouse takes on the role of "holding environment," or confidant. Although having a loving spouse may be the best option, this role can also be taken up by close friends. For many, true happiness is felt while in the company of good friends.

We often draw great comfort from our friends when times are tough. Because friends help us work our way through the obstructions of life, they're instrumental in creating happy moments. They also serve as a kind of supplemental memory bank, helping us recall experiences and things about ourselves, including happy memories, that we've forgotten. They affect our physical well-being as well: research has shown that having someone to confide in reduces stress, strengthens the immune system, and boosts longevity. Talking about intimate things—engaging in self-disclosure—has great prophylactic value. Sigmund Freud, when he started to experiment with psychoanalysis, referred to the process of having people talk about whatever came to mind (unscreened by the normal conventions of daily life) as "the talking cure."

Making friends isn't easy for most of us, unfortunately. Friendship isn't something we can buy in a store or create with a wish or a snap of the fingers. Building a friendship—and that includes a relationship with a partner—requires hard work and determination. We have to make an effort to understand and help others, giving a part of ourselves away in the process. And if we think only of ourselves—if we engage in excessive narcissistic behavior—it's very difficult to establish real friendships.

The groundwork for most friendships is laid early in life—during childhood, high school, and university. Friendships develop so easily in our youth that we take the whole process for granted. But *keeping* friends—that's another story; it doesn't occur the least bit automatically. Keeping a friendship going, helping it to develop and mature rather than allowing it to stagnate, is a delicate process. Friendships are fragile entities that require care, nurturance, and even sacrifice. Maintaining friendships involves being loyal, affectionate, sympathetic, and ready to help when the need arises. But we're amply repaid for our efforts: *having* a friend means ready access to a willing ear, an understanding heart, and a helping hand. As a caveat it can be said that a person's character can often be assessed in the selection of his or her friends.

What happens to our friendships as we grow older? Do the crucial links we made early in life remain intact, or do we lose sight of the people who once were our friends? For many people the answer to this latter question is affirmative. And yet despite the fact that friendships are often very transitional, they become increasingly important as we age. In middle age and onward, they're needed more than ever before. Unfortunately, for many of us the opportunity to make new friendships seems to diminish after the early stages in life. As a result, the friends we lose aren't replaced.

And lose them we do. Sometimes distance separates us; sometimes our interests diverge; sometimes one of us outgrows the other; sometimes we drift apart for lack of effort. Even marriage can be a factor in the dissolution of other friendships. If the marriage bond is particularly intense, all others may pale in comparison. Furthermore, the exclusivity of a partnership may bring out negative feelings such as jealousy. A spouse may look at the friend as a bad influence or find certain behaviors in the friend disturbing. When the chemistry isn't right between a partnered couple and a particular friend, a difficult choice has to be made. Having young children—with all the caretaking that this implies—may also hamper friendships. Taking care of kids often triggers an inward-looking pattern that leaves little time for the development of new friendships or the cultivation of old.

But not all friendships end deliberately. As we get older, death becomes a more frequent visitor, diminishing our circle of friendship against our will. All these various transformations point out the need to be active in maintaining friendships. Samuel Johnson coined it very appropriately: "If a man does not make new acquaintances as he advances through life, he will soon find himself left alone. A man should keep his friendships in constant repair." Since life doesn't stand still, we need to look forward, not just back. We need to be proactive in searching out people who would likely be compatible, showing an interest in them rather than waiting for them to show an interest in us. If we don't make an effort to establish new friendships, we may find ourselves all alone in old age—a situation that unbalances the happiness equation.

In dealing with people we're close to—partners, friends, neighbors, and colleagues—it's important to treat them as we'd like to be treated ourselves. The sage Confucius once said, "Behave toward everyone as if receiving a great guest." That's excellent advice. Being fair to others is important as we pass through life, partly because we inspire fairness in return. If we treat people well, it's likely that we'll be treated well by them; on the other hand, if we feel a sense of entitlement and demand special treatment from those around us, it's likely that we'll alienate loved ones, souring crucial relationships.

Giving fair treatment—that is, ensuring reciprocity in our relationships—requires the ability to place ourselves in another person's shoes. That's why true narcissists, with their unempathic outlook, have a hard time establishing real friendships. They simply can't imagine how it feels to be in someone else's situation. People with certain other personality disorders—those who are narcissistic, paranoid or schizoid, for example—shouldn't apply for friendship either, given their similar problems with empathy.

The reason empathy is such a critical element in interpersonal relationships is that life is a process of social exchange. People make calculations—though not necessarily consciously—about what they get out of every relationship. Given the principle of distributive justice and equity that's at work in every human interaction, what we put into a relationship and what we get out of it have to remain in equilibrium.

Something to Do

There's a cartoon from *The New Yorker* that shows an executive coming home from work, entering the house with his briefcase in his hands. His wife looks at him expectantly, as if having asked him how his day went. The caption reads, "What kind of day it was? Well, it was a day like any other day. I loved, I hated. I laughed, I cried. I felt pain, I inflicted pain. I made friends, I made enemies ..."

As the cartoon suggests, work, the second pillar of happiness, ties a person to the human community. It adds purpose to our living. It stimulates the senses. That's why work is essential for our mental health. People who have nothing meaningful to do tend to be unhappy. Paradoxically, the hardest work of all may be doing nothing.

Consider Oblomov, a prime example of impaired work performance. This tragic tale of passivity, apathy, and indolence, as told by the nineteenth-century Russian novelist Ivan Goncharov, has retained its powerful imagery to the present day. Oblomov is an exemplar of arrested character development, an individual incapable of going beyond a functionally vegetative state. Sapped by passivity and apathy, he found life too challenging—but so was suicide. Oblomov never really lived his life at all (or what we think life is supposed to be). He simply stayed in bed. (Of course, one could argue that bed is exactly the place to be if one wants to avoid risk. On the other hand, most deaths take place in bed!) Oblomov replaced real action with daydreams and fantasies, transferring to the reader his own sense of impending doom and futility. While Oblomov's is an extreme case, it warns us of possible consequences of the passivity and inertia that we may fear in ourselves. Work in and of itself isn't the answer, however. Doing work that brings no satisfaction is likewise very draining. As the writer Maxim Gorky once said, "When work is pleasure, life is a joy. When work is duty, life is slavery."

One of the best prizes in life is the opportunity to work at something we like and are challenged by. Unfortunately, far too often, for far too many of us, work is drudgery. Workplaces take on the appeal of concentration camps. While economic necessity forces some people into work that they find meaningless, many of us can afford to be selective. Unless we find ourselves unable to climb out of that first category, we need to stick with the good stuff and trim off the useless branches, focusing on work that we can do well and that makes us feel really alive.

If happiness is a goal, we should also look for work that gives us a sense of purpose. When we feel that what we do makes a difference, our life has more meaning. Work that allows us to feel that we're making a contribution, work that really absorbs us, work that demands our total concentration—this is the kind of work that makes for happy moments (and thus creates happy memories to sustain us in difficult times). If we completely lose our sense of time when we're working and don't find ourselves fatigued at the end of the day, that's a good indicator that we're doing this kind of work. As a German proverb says, "When a man is happy, he doesn't hear the clock strike." Psychologist Mihaly Csikszentmihalyi uses the label "flow" for the beyond-time-and-surroundings feeling that meaningful work brings.

As important as meaningful work is, however, it's not as crucial as close relationships. Even the person who spends every day waiting for the five o'clock whistle to blow may consider himself happy if he has a loving family and good friends to spend his free time with.

Something to Hope for

Finally, we all need hope in our lives; we need something to strive for. Meaningful work is one of the ways in which we create hope. But there are many other routes to take. Hope is a vital element of the human condition, spurring us on and encouraging us to explore and grow. As we go through the process of discovery that each life is, the makeup of our desires—the profile of our hope—is the only real boundary we face. Thus the way we cultivate or abandon hope is an important part of our "inner theatre," a key element in the script of life.

Though we tend to think of hope as something ephemeral, it can also be tangible. It can take on many forms—a new love affair, an exciting job opportunity, the building of a dream house, a special trip. There's something for everybody. The images attached to hope are registered with the other good memories that sustain us when times are tough.

Because hope is linked to meaningful goals and objectives, it points us toward a (gradually evolving) destination. (I'll say more about this later.) Hope gives us a sense of direction in our journey through life—a sense of where we want to go. In fact, without hope, why undertake the journey at all? With despair at the helm, we might end up somewhere we don't want to be. Hope takes the edge off melancholy and despondency and helps us to remember that the sun is always there above the clouds, even if we can't see it.

People who have hope have an easier time dealing with the misfortunes that are part and parcel of life's journey. They look at setbacks as temporary states, not permanent conditions. They get new strength out of the fact that they see each adversity as limited in time. They don't despair. They are persistent; they don't easily give up.

We can reframe the concept of hope by referring to *dreams*. Because dreams give life meaning, emptiness and despair flourish in their absence. A life without dreams is little more than death. And yet our dreams often seem distant; they hover in the sunshine, tempting but elusive. Often they truly *are* beyond our grasp. But even if we're never able to touch our dreams, we can look up to them and believe in them, and try to live our life accordingly. Thus our dreams can spur us on to higher and better things. Without dreams, we might just as well operate on automatic pilot, leading a life without poetry or joy.

The most impressive feats in the world have been accomplished by people who've had dreams—*big* dreams. But to be able to dream, we have to believe in ourselves. We have to have faith that what we aspire to be, we *can* be. When we look at individuals who've made a difference in the world—famous dreamers such as Mahatma Gandhi, Martin Luther King, Jr., Mother Teresa, and Nelson Mandela—we see the evidence of dreams that gradually crystallized over time, enduring regardless of obstacles. These dreamers envisioned lofty ways to create a better world—and then set about realizing their dreams, one step at a time.

The example of these individuals tells us that we should hold on to the dreams of our youth, or at least retain our willingness to dream the way we did then—to aim for the stars, transcending what others think is possible. After all, if we aim for the stars, we might at least hit the moon! But dreams are delicate flowers, easily crushed. That's the reason many of us find it difficult to talk about our dreams, to share them with others. We wonder whether people will laugh at us, deride us, consider us fools. And yet that's a risk we need to take. If we dare to share our dreams with a selected few people we trust, those loved ones can help us hold on to our dreams. Even if our worst fears come true and our dreams are dismissed as foolish, we need to pursue them relentlessly, for in that pursuit lies our chance for happiness. We're the architects of our own ambitions. We're happy as a result of our own efforts once we know what course to take. Dreams are our possibilities. We need to use all our talent and energy and courage to fulfill those dreams.

Unfortunately, there's a dark side to dreams as well. Excessively high aspirations, as symbolized in these kinds of dreams, can be as great a threat to happiness as a lack of such dreams is. When challenges consistently exceed our abilities, we become stressed. If the discrepancy between where we are and where we'd like to be or where we feel we ought to be is too high, we may become depressed and unhappy. If we stop worrying about things that are beyond the power of our will, however, we'll feel much better. Thus, as a practical piece of advice, it's often better to break big dreams down into manageable parts. Think big thoughts but enjoy the small pleasures. Doing so allows for a sense of control and lets us celebrate small milestones along the way.

For example, if a publisher asks me to write a book and suggests that it should run to about three hundred pages, it seems like a daunting assignment. But if I break that assignment into manageable parts and resolve to write three pages a day, the task is more manageable. I feel good about myself each day when I've fulfilled that specific commitment. And earlier than I had expected, the book is ready to be handed in to the publisher. Nothing is impossible if we divide it into small jobs. In any case, the process of moving toward our dreams may be more important to the feeling of happiness than reaching that goal.

People without dreams feel disoriented, drifting restlessly through life. Sometimes only an enforced challenge such as a life-threatening accident, a serious illness, or a war can save them. Paradoxical as it sounds, such events give people a new lease on life because they force a hard look at reality. People who have come through such circumstances often reset their priorities, reestablish floundering relationships, and identify and pursue meaningful tasks and commitments. Drifters thus are given a new beginning, and happiness may follow.

One of my students described to me how he was almost crushed under the debris during a bomb explosion in a hotel in Lebanon during the internecine war that took place in that country. He had been a rather confused, happy-go-lucky drifter until this experience, which transformed him. Getting out of the rubble relatively unscathed made him really appreciate being alive. He felt as if he had been reborn. Having become a "twice born" (to quote the psychologist William James), he rearranged his priorities. He felt that he had been given a new chance in life and didn't want to waste any more time. He returned to his medical studies, became a physician, and turned into a major AIDS activist, spending most of his time in Africa implementing preventive programs.

Even if we firmly believe in our own efficacy, pursuing our dreams can be daunting. Those dreams can seem so formidable, and our powers so slight. But life is made up of little things. When we tackle our dreams step by step, they're achievable. The sage Lao-Tzu said, "The journey of a thousand miles begins with one step." The greatest things ever done in life have been done little by little. Our initial efforts, paltry though they may seem, can turn into big things later. Those tentative first steps point us in the right direction and color the rest of the journey.

6

STRIKING THE
RIGHT BALANCE

*I have measured out my life with
coffee spoons.*
T. S. ELIOT

*What I dream of is an art of balance,
of purity and serenity devoid of troubling
or depressing subject matter...
a soothing, calming influence on the mind,
something like a good armchair which provides
relaxation from physical fatigue.*
HENRI MATISSE

Happiness is no laughing matter.
RICHARD WHATELY

Even when we have people we love, work that's meaningful, and hope to sustain us, happiness can be elusive if we fail to keep our private and public lives in balance. Achieving balance sounds like a simple goal, but it's easier said than done. The pressures of the workplace can be tremendous. Because the corporate culture of many organizations negates family values, those pressures affect not only the employee but also the family. And as if workplace pressures weren't enough, we're apt to throw in a few self-inflicted ones! We may be trapped in a career maze, for example, obsessed with beating out our office competitors for the next step in the career trajectory. And yet when we confuse happiness with success—at least the outward version of success, as represented by wealth, position, power, or fame— we all but guarantee that the various components in our life will be thrown out of joint (though the unbalancing process can be so insidious that we don't realize what's happening).

Living a Whole Life Versus a Deferred Life

The fact that many of us are masters of self-delusion, having a great capacity for rationalization and intellectualization, adds to the disequilibrium between private and public life. We try to fool ourselves into believing that we're well balanced. For example, most people, when asked how much time they spend at home, give an answer that's far from reality (though they don't necessarily distort the facts *consciously*). And even those who are aware of the disproportionate time they spend at the office may console themselves by referring to their non-work time as "quality" time. They may try to convince themselves that it's not the length of time they spend at home with the family that counts, but rather the intensity, the quality of that time. But do they really believe what they say? And would the other members of their family agree with their conclusions?

I often hear businessmen comment that they're working very hard now so that their wife and children will have a better life later. (My apologies for using the male gender, but most often it's men who make such a comment.) All too frequently, however, when this infamous later date arrives, there's no longer a wife. She's moved in with someone else, and the children have become strangers. They call another man Daddy and don't really know their father anymore. All that the dedicated worker gets for following the build-for-the-future, deferred-life strategy is isolation and loneliness. It seems to be so much easier to make a success of *oneself* than to make a success of *one's life*. We can get A's in all our courses but flunk life!

We need to remind ourselves, as we strive for that first kind of success—the kind which, as a Yiddish proverb says, "makes you drunk without wine"—that certain important moments won't ever be back. We need to cherish those passing moments; we need to seize the day. Life isn't a rehearsal; it's the real thing. If we want to enjoy life, we have to do it *today,* not tomorrow or some faraway time in the future. We have to ask ourselves what we really want. Do we want a *whole* life or a *deferred* life?

Many investment bankers I've worked with have struggled with this choice. Some of them, because of hardships experienced at an impressionable period in their lives, made the deliberate career decision early on never to be poor again. Their main goal in life was financial independence. Through extremely hard work, they succeeded in meeting that target, often acquiring money beyond their wildest dreams. To quote one person: "I earned more money in one year than my father did his whole life."

People caught in this bind are like rats on a treadmill, unable to get off. As they meet the initial need for financial security, new needs—mostly imagined—begin to emerge. They want a bigger house, a more exclusive sports car, a special summerhouse. The usual vacations don't suffice any longer; more luxurious getaways are required. Their "toys" get more expensive as well. The more they have, the more they want, not realizing that happiness doesn't cost anything. Oh, they mumble that they're soon going to stop working, that they're soon going to pursue the things they've always wanted to do. Sometime in the future,

when they have more time, they'll once more take piano lessons, for example; sometime in the future, they'll go back to university to do art history; sometime in the future, they'll take up painting. But that moment never seems to come around. And in the meantime, life is passing them by. Even if their work is exciting, they're leading a one-dimensional life. There's no time for anything *but* work. Such people have mortgaged the present for the future (or so they hope).

Sometimes we *want* to live for today but feel that we don't have the luxury of that choice. Perhaps there's an overseas trip that just can't be missed if we want to be promoted—though it means missing a son's birthday. Or a presentation that has to be made (and made well) if we hope to boost our sagging sales figures—though it conflicts with a daughter's tennis competition. These are difficult choices, to be sure, especially with a job or career on the line. But the family is on the line as well. Kids grow up and leave home quickly enough. Before we know it, we no longer have any influence in their lives; they make their own decisions without consulting us. And if we were seldom with them in their early years, what will our legacy be? How will they remember us? What will they say at our funeral (and what would we have *liked* them to say)?

A fulfilling life is meaningless unless it's coined in the present. Far too many of us fail to live for today. And yet if we put all our energy into reaching out for the future, that which is now in our grasp will be lost! Nothing matches the pain of realizing the full importance of time only when there's very little of it left.

The most important influence on the life of any child is the parents, who shape character and values through personal guidance and unconscious suggestion. How can we help our children grow up as well-rounded adults if we're not there? How can we instill values if we're always at the office? How can we give our children meaningful memories if we're too busy to spend time with them? The bottom line: despite all the fantasies about quality time, meaningful relationships imply *sustained* relationships.

With organizations as demanding as today's typically are, we have to be firm in setting boundaries in order to preserve those aspects of life that are truly important. Perhaps if enough people speak up, in this age of the knowledge worker, employers will have no choice but to make the proper adjustments. And even if we have to take a solitary stand on this issue, our efforts at balancing life are an investment in the future. As a wit once pointed out, no one on his or her deathbed has ever been overheard to say, "I should have spent more time at the office." Having special moments with family members is critical to the attainment of happiness. Furthermore, being able to look back at these moments with happiness is to enjoy life twice.

Outward Success Versus Inner Success

Albert Einstein had a formula for success that says a lot about balance—$A = X + Y + Z$—where A stands for success, X stands for work, Y stands for play, and Z stands for keeping one's mouth shut. Like Freud with his formula of love and work, Einstein pointed out some of the essentials that affect happiness.

No person will ever know true happiness without having a few successes to his or her credit. Success creates a feeling of competence, a sense that one is capable of creatively addressing the demands of any situation. A satisfactory self-evaluation depends on meeting personal or group-determined standards. In other words, it relies on comparison against an explicit or implicit goal. However, successful accomplishment of a specific goal or broad dream doesn't *guarantee* happiness. The destination we reach after months or years of striving may turn out to be a disappointment. That discovery can plunge us into despair, if we let it, or it can prompt us to embark on a *new* journey—a journey that will foster meaning and happiness.

True happiness depends on our coming to grips with feelings of inner restlessness and anxiety resulting from self-imposed perceptions of a discrepancy between where we are and where we would like to be—that is, the comparison between our aspirations and our actual achievements. And for many of us that discrepancy looms large. The fact is, we *won't* all be CEOs; we *won't* all discover the cure for cancer—and we need to accept that. Our success needs to be measured not by what we've achieved but by the obstacles we've overcome. Furthermore, as mentioned earlier, we need to celebrate the small victories along the way.

Many of us tend to focus on outward success—the kind equated with wealth, position, power, and fame; we think that happiness consists of *having* and *getting*. But pursuing those goals is like chasing a rainbow. All we see when we arrive is a gray mist. What makes for happiness is *inner* success—the kind that results from living life to the fullest. Einstein's play and active listening to others (a corollary of his holding the tongue) are essential to inner success, because they help us to acquire precious possessions such as friendship, love, goodness, concern, kindness, and wisdom. The success that really satisfies—that contributes to moments of happiness—often comes to people who aren't looking for success. That's because the road to true success is off the beaten path.

Not only is the outward success ephemeral; it's downright dangerous. I firmly believe that the unrelenting pursuit of outward success is one of today's chief sources of unhappiness. An obsession with success can have serious dysfunctional consequences, because it snowballs: people driven by success are rarely satisfied, no matter how high they climb; *no* accomplishment gives lasting satisfaction. Whenever they reach one level of success, they imagine yet another, higher level. The income they once dreamed of, for example, now looks like a starvation salary. It comes down to this: people who equate happiness with success will never achieve *enough* success to be happy. They're like Sisyphus, interminably pushing a rock up a hill. Ironically, Sisyphus's only period of happiness was probably that short moment when the rock was rolling down—when he wasn't pushing, when he had time for self-reflection. But self-reflection would probably have been the last thing he'd have wanted. His conclusions would have been depressing indeed.

The inner restlessness and discontent that accompany the pursuit of external success have ruined many a person. Paradoxically, happiness rests on being satisfied *both with what we have and what we don't have.* That dual satisfaction is a solid foundation for a feeling of well-being. The happiest people are often those who don't want things they can't get—who like their present state.

7
PUTTING THINGS
IN PERSPECTIVE

Envy never makes holiday.
FRANCIS BACON

Fools may our scorn, not envy raise,
For envy is a kind of praise.
JOHN GAY

The neighbor's cooking always smells better.
MALTESE PROVERB

An important ingredient in the recipe for happiness is comparison, though too much of that essential ingredient can sour the stew. Let's look at the ways comparison can further or hinder our happiness.

Putting things in perspective, regularly reminding ourselves that our life isn't that bad after all, helps to keep unhappiness at bay. This healthy process can involve both intrapsychic comparison (whereby we compare our present state to a past, less desirable state) and interpersonal comparison. We might, for example, be grateful when our car breaks down that now we have the money to pay for repairs (whereas ten years ago we would have had to abandon the clunker). Or we might, when facing surgery, be grateful that we have someone to hold our hand (unlike our solitary elderly neighbor). In other words, when we feel low, we may visualize past stressful situations, or others' stressful situations, to make us feel better. Reminding ourselves of how bad things could be in comparison with our comparatively more comfortable day-to-day existence—a universal and constructive way to boost morale—generally raises our spirits.

There are both upward and downward comparisons, of course. Things aren't *always* better than they used to be, and we're not *always* healthier or better paid or smarter than our neighbor. In general, however, happy people make more downward comparisons than upward. No matter what their situation, they can see others who have it worse, which helps them realize how well off they really are. They've learned to appreciate the things they have rather than dwelling on what others have—a lesson they probably mastered with their ABCs. Perhaps when, as children, they complained about feeling disadvantaged in some way, their parents gave them examples of other people who were worse off.

While unhappy people inevitably make both upward and downward comparisons in assessing their life situation, it's the upward comparisons they dwell on. Feeling a deep sense of having been wronged, they spend their days searching for confirmation that life has given them a poor hand of cards. As a result, the selection of targets to compare themselves with is biased. By primarily making comparisons upward, they focus on the fact that others have a better deal in life. *Why does my neighbor have a better car than I have? How does my sister manage to go on such expensive vacations?* When occasionally they focus on someone who is worse off than they are, they savor that sensation, but their "pleasure" is quickly overshadowed by the envy of the many others who are perceived as having gotten a much better deal in life.

People fixated on the idea of having been given a bad deal see one person's gain as the other person's loss. They look at everything as a zero-sum game. Regardless of what they're in pursuit of—be it love, power, or money—they're always able to find someone who appears to be better off, and they see that other person as hoarding what should rightfully be theirs.

All of us feel disadvantaged at times, particularly when we compare ourselves to others a few steps up the ladder in status, looks, income, or power. Our challenge is to work through our mixed emotions. For the purposes of mental health, it's important not to dwell on negative comparisons, not to become obsessed by a sense of having been wronged. Otherwise, envy rears its ugly head and threatens to devour us.

Social comparison and envy are part of a single continuum. The former shades gradually into the latter, which brings out the worst in people. Bertrand Russell recognized this when he said, "Few people can be happy unless they hate some other person, nation, or creed." We should ask ourselves, though, if *happy* is the right adjective to use in such a situation. Russell continued his discussion by stating, "If you desire glory, you may envy Napoleon. But Napoleon envied Caesar, Caesar envied Alexander, and Alexander, I daresay, envied Hercules, who never existed."

As I indicated earlier, some people find a kind of enjoyment in other people's misery. Those same people favor upward comparison, which generally triggers an envious, hostile reaction. That reaction isn't entirely other-directed, however. As Hermann Hesse observed, "If we hate a person, we hate something in our image of him that lies within ourselves. What is not within ourselves does not upset us." As Hesse clearly understood, envious people have serious problems centered on self-esteem. They're more unhappy with themselves than they are with those others they deride.

I doubt that there's a person alive who, at one time or another, hasn't been troubled by envy—that is, by the painful or resentful awareness of an advantage enjoyed by someone else (such as wealth, power, status, love, or beauty) combined with the desire to possess that advantage. Envy is a truly universal emotion. And envy spawns a range of equally painful emotions: frustration, anger, self-pity, greed, spite, and vindictiveness. While acting out of envy may give temporary relief, any of these negative emotions can cause substantial subjective distress. Envy and all its offshoots are dangerous to self and others; they take prisoner those who indulge in them.

Not that people reveal or verbalize such feelings—not *deliberately* anyway. Envy isn't an emotion for public consumption. We prefer to hide it or at least dress it up in lofty imagery. Although envy has a positive side—it can be a great equalizer, reducing differences and reinforcing a sense of equity in relationships—too often it leads people to demand an eye for an eye. The result? One more blind person in a world already full of suffering.

St. Thomas Aquinas listed envy as one of the seven deadly sins. The Bible is certainly full of stories about envy. The Old Testament's ten commandments, for example, include "Thou shall not covet." Literature also has ample examples of envy, probably the best known being John Milton's portrait of Satan in *Paradise Lost.* In that depiction, Satan is a fallen angel who, seething with envy and wanting revenge, fabricates man's fall from Paradise. The universal nature of envy is also attested to in the proverbs of many different societies: for example, in Bulgaria, "Other people's eggs have two yolks"; in Denmark, "If envy were a fever, all the world would be ill"; in Sweden, the expression "royal Swedish envy" (warning against provoking envy by being too conspicuous); in various countries, the "tall poppy

syndrome" (highlighting the enjoyment people seem to get out of the downfall of "tall poppies").

The most dramatic story concerning envy that I know of is Russian. It concerns a peasant to whom God granted the fulfillment of any wish. There was, however, a catch. Whatever the peasant chose, God would do twice as much for his neighbor. The idea that his neighbor would be better off then he was, whatever he did, troubled him. After mulling over the offer, the peasant finally said, "Take out one of my eyes." The novelist Gore Vidal (in a moment of self-analysis) presents that same dynamic quite cynically in his comment, "Whenever a friend succeeds, a little something in me dies." Elsewhere he says, "It is not enough to succeed; others must fail."

Sometimes envy is packaged (and successfully disguised) as moral indignation. We pretend to be very righteous about people who we claim have transgressed some kind of moral code—denouncing, for example, a colleague for living ostentatiously in a world plagued by poverty. This sense of righteousness very often masks a desire to be in the transgressor's situation, however. When people obsess over the "despicable" behavior of someone else, they may well be tempted by that very behavior. The target of their wrath may represent what they most fear in themselves.

The indiscretions of a number of television preachers in America are good illustrations. Certain televangelists have preached about vice and sin, about avarice and greed, while at the same time visiting prostitutes and misusing the money given to them by their constituencies. The book *Elmer Gantry* by Sinclair Lewis (later filmed as a movie in which Burt Lancaster gave a masterful performance) is the story of a preacher who is a con man, but it's also an attack on the ignorant, gross, and predatory leaders who had crept into the Protestant Church. The novel describes how Elmer Gantry, a "God-fearing" man, preached sin and damnation by day, and then by night engaged in the same activities he had earlier condemned. Thus moral indignation is often envy with a halo. To quote the filmmaker Vittorio de Sica, "Moral indignation is in most cases two percent moral, forty-eight percent indignation, and fifty percent envy."

Ambrose Bierce, in *The Devil's Dictionary*, touches dramatically on the destructiveness of envy when he describes happiness as an "agreeable sensation arising from contemplating the misery of another." The German language includes the word *Schadenfreude*, meaning pleasure at the misery of others. But if a person bases his or her happiness on enjoying the misery of others, what does that say about the overall quality of that life? Although the misery of others can bring moments of pleasure, true happiness can't coexist with envy, spite, or vindictiveness. If envy takes a person prisoner, it limits human potential, makes for disconnectedness, stifles the ability to play, and leads to unhappiness.

8
COPING WITH STRESS

Don't remain a dependent, malleable patient:
Become your own soul's doctor.
EPICTETUS

The trouble with being in the rat race is that
even if you win, you're still a rat.
LILY TOMLIN

A heart attack is nature's way of telling us to slow down.
PROVERB

Albert Schweitzer once said that happiness is nothing more than good health and a poor memory. While his comment about poor memory may meet with objections—after all, who wants to be accused of being in a state of denial?—monitoring health is undeniably important. If we don't protect our health, the attainment of happiness is an impossible pursuit. When all is said and done, our physical condition strongly influences (and in some cases even determines) our mental state. According to many stress researchers, physical state is a strong predictor of happiness, particularly for the old. It may be old hat to say so, but the ego is first and foremost a *bodily* ego. It's hard to think clearly when we're in poor physical condition. As a result, when we're assailed by ill health, our thoughts and conversations tend to be limited to a discussion about our various physical ailments. At times, all of us have encountered people who converse only in somatic language—the language of bodily concerns.

Being healthy can be compared to burning a candle wisely. If we take excellent care of our candle, it burns for a long time. If we start to mess with it, it can go up in smoke in a very short time. Unfortunately, in my dealings with executives I've met quite a few people with the habit of burning the candle at both ends—anger-prone, Type-A people. They experience a sense of great time-urgency, they're restless, impatient, and extremely competitive, and they possess a high level of aggressiveness and free-floating hostility. This constellation of behaviors is a major risk factor in coronary heart disease.

You may know the kind of people I'm talking about. They're like rats on a treadmill or the rabbit in *Alice in Wonderland*—always in a hurry and never getting to their destination. Do you recognize the type? (Do you perhaps recognize *yourself?*) When these people go to a restaurant, they eat fast, talk fast, and pay the bill fast. They have no time to enjoy their meal. They certainly don't linger over wine or coffee. Their speech is loud, at times even explosive; their face muscles are tense. Poor listeners, they always try to dominate the conversation. Because they're under constant pressure (whether self-induced or external), they feel guilty when they attempt to relax. In fact, whenever possible they do more than one thing at a time. Even during the night they're not at peace. They may, for example, grind their teeth in accompaniment to stressful dream imagery—a pastime that's made many a dentist happy.

Physical health can be compared to a bank account. This is an unusual account, however—one from which we can only withdraw; the bank doesn't allow deposits. Some people tend to be spendthrifts. Unable to save, they squander their health as readily as they do their money, committing suicide slowly. They realize the importance of their health only when there's very little of it left.

Stress researchers sometimes make a distinction between physiological and chronological age. For some—the candle-burners and bank-account raiders—physiological age overtakes chronological age. Since physiological age is to some extent within our control, we need to monitor our health vigilantly—exercising regularly, eating sensibly, drinking only in moderation, and recognizing what smoking and drugs can do to us.

Furthermore, we need to remember that, while old age will come to all of us (at least to the lucky ones), our so-called golden years will be brighter if we've managed throughout our life to maintain a low-stress, positive state of mind. People under stress are more susceptible to illness. Findings from the field of psychoneuroimmunology indicate that pleasurable experiences and positive states of mind enhance the immune system. It appears that our body's immune system fights disease more effectively when we're happy. As a result, happier people live longer. Worry, lack of physical and emotional contact, anger, and hostility, on the other hand, are hazardous to our health. Thus negative moods encourage illness.

Of course, there's more to physical health than taking practical steps toward fitness. Some of us have had bad luck with genetic inheritance, for example; others have had the misfortune to be tapped by a disease that vigilance couldn't have prevented. Still, far too many people mortgage their future, only to regret having done so later in life.

The American humorist P. J. O'Rourke once said, "There is one thing women can never take away from men. We die sooner." We can discern a moral underlying the humor of that remark: men would do well to adopt certain "female" characteristics—among them, emotional intimacy, which most people would concede women are better at than men. Social support—the sense of being liked and appreciated by friends and family members, the comfortable give-and-take of confidants—provides a buffer against stress and promotes happiness. Someone to talk to about intimate matters helps alleviate stressful situations. The people (men and women alike) most at risk for ill health and unhappiness are the ones who bear their problems alone, unable or unwilling to talk about what's troubling them. Fortunately, disclosure begets disclosure. When we express our fears to other people, they generally share their own concerns in turn, and we come to understand that we're not alone in our problems; others struggle with similar issues. For most of us that's a reassuring discovery. It leads to peace of mind.

Statistics tell us that people in close relationships tend to have better health-behavior practices. People who care about each other make an effort to monitor each other's health. When there's intimacy in a relationship, the partners tend to drink and smoke less, avoid drugs, have a better diet, and follow their doctor's orders.

Sexual activity can also counter stress. Not only does it have a positive effect on relationships, it also enhances physical fitness. If sex is mutually satisfying, it enhances self-esteem, works as an anti-depressant, and counters stress by boosting the immune system. In contrast, sex in the absence of loving sensations can negatively affect one's health and happiness. As the philosopher Epictetus said, "An active sex life within a framework of personal commitments augments the integrity of the people involved and is part of a flourishing life."

An optimistic mood state also serves as a buffer against stress, a fact that has been known to us for a long time. In the Old Testament book of Proverbs, we find King Solomon saying, "A merry heart doeth good like a medicine." Stress researchers concur with this finding. Laughter is an essential component of both mental and physical health. People who laugh often actually live longer. In his book

Anatomy of an Illness, the journalist Norman Cousins explained in great detail his theory that his recovery from a potentially life-threatening illness could be attributed to his active use of laughter. Laughter has a healing quality. Because laughter decreases stress hormones in the blood (such as adrenaline, epinephrine, and norepinephrine), it relaxes us, bringing us into a calmer, more homeostatic state. Laughter makes the body young and lively, exercises various organs, and (like positive mood states generally) increases our immune response.

We can laugh to forget, but we shouldn't forget to laugh. People who can't laugh are psychologically incomplete. Because laughter, that audible sign of transient happiness, is an antidote to anxiety and depression, it makes tough times more tolerable. The ability to laugh at ourselves is of special significance, guarding as it does against arrogance and pomposity. In fact, it's a good test of mental health.

Regular exercise is also essential to both physical health and happiness. We feel better, both physically and mentally, after doing exercise. We're in a more relaxed state of body and mind. When we exercise regularly, we reduce our stress level, enjoy more energy and stamina, strengthen the heart, and have better circulation, lower blood pressure, faster metabolism, and more resistance to life-threatening diseases. Furthermore, regular exercise lessens the odds of becoming depressed or burnt out. The old adage *Mens sana in corpore sano*—a sound mind in a sound body—contains a lot of truth. Many a time when we think we're sick, it's all in the mind.

9
HOMO LUDENS

All work and no play makes Jack a dull boy.
PROVERB

Men deal with life as children with their play,
Who first misuse, then cast their toys away.
WILLIAM COWPER

Why not go out on a limb?
Isn't that where the fruit is?
FRANK SCULLY

One of these sunny afternoons I was walking over the "Pont des Arts" (the Arts Bridge) in Paris. The bridge was like a beehive of activity. There was this special buzz in the air. A sense of excitement and enthusiasm permeated the whole area. People—old and young—were everywhere: sitting, standing, and lying down. All of them were painting or commenting on each other's paintings. In the typical French proclivity for wordplay, it was "'Faites de la peinture," which literally means "painting activities." But the same text could also be read like, "Fête de la peinture," which is pronounced exactly in the same way but means "painting party." Looking at the scene, one could see how all these people were totally entranced cognitively, emotionally, and sensually. And that is what play is all about. While playing, we lose ourselves; interior and exterior worlds merge. We transform as a person. We loosen the baggage of daily life. A fusion occurs between childhood and adulthood. And on the bridge, the usual separation between children and grown-ups dissipated. They were all "playing" together.

In formulating his equation for happiness, Einstein was correct in pointing out the importance of play in our lives. Play is closely tied to creativity; it also has a regenerative function. Play implies doing things outside of our normal routine, a diversification of interests. As the saying goes, all work and no play makes for a dull person. We gather happy life experiences (and therefore memories) by having a variety of interests. Leisure activities serve a revitalizing function. As mentioned earlier, research results have shown that people who enjoy leisure tend to be happier. Leisure helps us to look at old situations in new ways. Real recreation (that's re-creation) stimulates aspiration and makes us more innovative and effective at work and in our relationships.

Many people don't know how to manage leisure; they don't know how to be playful. An executive in one of my leadership seminars was just such a man. Listening to his story, I had a flashback to the paintings of Diego Velázquez (the most important Spanish painter of the 17th century), which featured children who looked eerily adult. This executive, who in childhood was always treated like an adult, could have stepped out of such a painting. He had been forced into an adult role prematurely because of a depressed mother and a father who had disappeared when he was two years old. With no other support figure around, this man had assumed a responsible role in the family at an early age. In that role he became the confidant to his mother, trying to help her overcome her dark moments and sharing her emotional burdens. As he grew older, he increasingly took care of household duties. Meanwhile, his childhood slipped away. Like the children in Velázquez's paintings, he never got the opportunity to play, to engage in make-believe.

As an adult he focused on his work, becoming a very successful businessman. His colleagues and subordinates described him as quite caring but too serious. Unfortunately, he compartmentalized his caring, saving it for the office. At home he was detached from his wife and son, probably in reaction to having been overinvolved with his mother in the past. Having relegated the childrearing to his wife, he remained so distant from his son that the young man became like a stranger to him. When alone with his son, he felt awkward, uncomfortable; he didn't know what to say or how to handle himself. When I first met this man, late in his life, he was trying to pick up the broken thread of his childhood, trying to make a belated effort at play.

While some people—this executive among them—don't know how to play, dedicating all their energy to work, others play too hard and too much. But does life have to be either/or? I don't think so. We increase the probability of attaining happiness when we learn to find play at work and learn to work at play. Well-balanced personalities don't work all the time. They know how to laugh; they know how to play; they know how to do fun things with others.

When we play—even when we play at work—we return to the world of childhood. Once more we experience the feelings of joy, surprise, and anticipation that make up the world of an infant. We again feel as alive, as intense, as we did when we were young. We enter a world where time doesn't matter, a world of fantasy, of daydreams and night dreams.

Playing can be viewed as a constructive form of regression. (Some psychoanalysts call it regression in the service of the ego.) It's in the transitional world of play—the domain that floats between make-believe and reality, between teddy bears and adult responsibilities—where creative processes take place. It's a world of intuition, of free association, of metaphors and images, of imagination without limits—in short, a world of infinite possibilities. It's a world of divergent thinking, leading to connections and associations that contribute to new insights. When adults are in this world of play, periods of private, creative inner work alternate with experiences of reality testing, illumination, and reintegration. We need to realize that minds are like parachutes, they work better when they are open! Getting into such a state of mind enables us to deal in new ways with questions, issues, sensibilities, and problems that have left us puzzled. While we're playing, while we're doing things out of the ordinary, solutions emerge that have eluded the traditional work approach. Such creative insights often make for intense moments of happiness.

Given the importance of play for creativity and happiness, each of us should evaluate our ability to engage in it. Do we ever question things that have long been taken for granted at work? Are there things that really fire us up at the office? Do we have any passions outside work? Do we engage in activities that tap other parts of our brains? Are we in touch with the crazy side of ourselves? Do we daydream and pay attention to our night dreams? The more affirmation we can give to this set of questions, the better off we are. Taking a playful approach to job responsibilities fosters creativity, while engaging in after-work hobbies and pursuits improves our outlook toward life and reenergizes our spirit (whether we opt for relatively tame activities such as fly-fishing, bird-watching, or the cultivation of roses, or venture into the likes of helicopter-skiing).

If diversity of leisure is absent, we may be in for a big surprise when retirement comes and our options are limited by physical and situational changes. I've known quite a few single-minded people, men and women whose only interests were career-related, who were at a complete loss upon retirement. While working, they never thought to seek pleasure outside the office. Their development as a person

was totally career-related. When they left the workplace in late middle age, they experienced a sense of abandonment and isolation, becoming disoriented and depressed and experiencing a variety of other stress symptoms. Some even died prematurely, discovering that having made no time for leisure, they had to make time for illness.

The growth that human beings experience through play is closely related to their exploratory need—the need on which cognition and learning are based. The developmental psychologist Robert White calls this need *competence motivation*. Although infants are born conspicuously incompetent, they are "programmed" not only to learn a great deal about their environment but also to find ways to affect and manipulate it. He (and other developmental psychologists) view exploratory behavior as a basic motivational need, the purpose of which is to acquire competence in dealing with the environment. The successes that are attained during that acquisition contribute to feelings of efficacy, which enhance significantly a person's sense of self-esteem.

This exploratory motivational need is manifested soon after birth. Child observation studies report that novelty, as well as the discovery of the effects of certain actions, stimulate the brain cells in infants and causes a prolonged state of attentive arousal. Similar reactions to opportunities for exploration continue into and throughout adulthood. Closely tied to the need for exploration is the need for self-assertion— the need to be able to choose what to do. Playful exploration and manipulation of the environment in response to exploratory-assertive motivation produces a sense of effectiveness and competency, of autonomy, initiative, and industry.

Understanding this basic motivational need makes us realize that learning shouldn't be seen as something we do only as preparation for adult life. On the contrary, the learning process should never stop. We need to continue developing our potential, growing and expanding as individuals. We need to be open to new challenges and tasks at different points in the lifespan.

As we look around us, we see a world that's in constant flux; new things are happening all the time. With all these changes, there are myriad discoveries waiting to be made. Ongoing learning means being passionately involved in life—attending to life's movements, sounds, and colors; using our senses of smell, taste, touch, hearing, and sight; cultivating our aesthetic side; and being adventurous.

What we learn in formal educational environments is important. Frequently, though, it's the studying done *after* school that has the greatest impact. In fact, many things that need to be learned simply can't be taught. Those things we learn by doing—and we remember them as a consequence. The recall factor of experiential learning is much greater than that of classroom learning, because the memories of critical incidents in life's course remain prominent.

The paradox of wisdom is that the more we learn, the more we discover how ignorant we are. That's not a bad thing: it's important to know how little we know. In fact, we should cherish our ignorance, because it's what pushes us toward further exploration. One of the secrets of a fulfilling life and the attainment of happiness is maintaining intellectual curiosity. But to be curious and learn, we also have to *un*learn; in other words, we have to be prepared to take risks, to go out on a limb. As the economist John Maynard Keynes once said, "The greatest difficulty in the world is not for people to accept new ideas but to make them forget about their old ideas."

All life throughout the universe is a process of growth and motion. We're no exception: we need to make a continuous effort to reshape ourselves. We also need to experiment. The more we do so, probing our limits and our surroundings, the more we develop. At times we'll fail at our endeavors. That's a guarantee. But temporary setbacks lead to learning experiences that are retained. Going out on a limb is well worth the risks. After all, the reason we go out on a limb is to harvest the fruits that grow there.

Nothing is interesting if we're not interested. The more things we're interested in, the more alive we are. It's a lonely person who thinks that he or she can no longer learn from others. That presumptuous stance is an invitation to disaster. Just as continuing to learn keeps us young, ceasing to learn hastens aging. In fact, nothing ages a person faster than not thinking, not exercising the brain. Few minds *wear* out; most rust away. Thus for our very survival we need to remain intellectually curious, striving for personal growth.

Our efforts to remain receptive to learning are made easier if we can retain certain qualities of childhood. Being playful, as mentioned earlier, helps us to see new circumstances as adventures. Being imaginative allows us to explore the vast, unmapped country within, that secret reservoir of promise and potential that few adults tap. Being creative permits us to use our imagination constructively, making use of childhood experiences recalled at will. Finally, being inquisitive brings us moments of happiness that stem from discovering new things. More often than not, the challenge isn't to arrive at new answers but to pose new questions. What we don't ask, we'll never know. The words *why* and *how* can't be used too often.

The joy of learning also helps us to become more effective teachers (and in that teaching process we learn ourselves). It's important, however, that we teach others *how* to think, not *what* to think. Generativity—the willingness to be a mentor and teacher to others, to really care for others—is an even more important factor as we grow older. Seeing young people who've been under our wings do well can bring moments of happiness, while envying the next generation stifles happiness.

François de la Rochefoucauld once wisely said, "The only thing constant in life is change." If we're open to learning, that ubiquitous change can be our teacher. In fact, since being mired in the rut of old habits leads to inflexibility and stagnation, we should not only *accept* change but seek it out, breaking routines and surprising ourselves and others. We need to let go of the past, realizing that today isn't yesterday. We need to keep trying new things and congratulate ourselves when we find ways to break the threatened monotony, find ways to be players, not spectators, in the game of life. It's better to be eighty years young than thirty years old. We grow old not by living but by losing interest in living.

10
THE QUEST FOR
AUTHENTICITY

|

Land of Heart's desire,
Where beauty has no ebb, decay no flood,
But joy is wisdom, Time an endless song.
WILLIAM YEATS ("THE LAND OF HEART'S DESIRE")

The art of being wise is the art of
knowing what to overlook.
WILLIAM JAMES

The happiness of your life depends
on the quality of your thoughts.
MARCUS AURELIUS

|

In pursuing happiness (as well as in dealing with all of life's vicissitudes), it's important to be authentic. It pays to be genuine, to be true to ourselves. If we're not honest with ourselves, how can we possibly be honest with other people? Authenticity implies a willingness to accept who we are and not attempt to pass for something or someone else. Authenticity means not only trusting our strengths but also facing our weaknesses and being patient with our imperfections. Authenticity also entails seeing others not as extensions of ourselves but as individuals in their own right, deserving of our respect.

While authenticity is grounded within, it affects all our interactions; it's like a diamond that scratches all other stones. If we're authentic, we inspire confidence in others. We heighten the spirits of those around us. We're empathic friends and good listeners. By paying attention to others—showing genuine concern—we provide "containment" and thereby create a "holding environment," that safe place that helps people to cope with conflict and anxiety. We're kind to others, nurturing the spirit of generosity, though we're humble about our efforts. We're at peace with ourselves and can therefore help others to feel better about themselves. (If we're *not* at peace with ourselves, how can we find or share peace elsewhere? If we *lack* confidence in ourselves, how can we inspire confidence in others?)

At the heart of authenticity is sincerity. If we're authentic, we abhor hypocrisy in self and others, and we're credible and trustworthy. In fact, it's authenticity that makes trust possible: the trust we put in ourselves permits us to have trust in others and to establish meaningful relationships. That trust also gives us the courage of our convictions in difficult situations, helping us to remain faithful to our values and beliefs. If we're authentic, we're the very embodiment of endurance and perseverance; we're not flags in the wind, changing with every pressure that comes along. Anyone can steer a boat when the sea is calm. It's in rough seas that the real helmsman—the authentic individual—emerges. Because adversity is a great teacher, peril is the scaffold on which self-reliance is built.

As we search for authenticity within ourselves, it's important to realize that if we're on a path without obstacles, it's probably a dead-end. The best lessons are learned not through successes but through failures. Surmounting difficulties hardens us for future struggles. Authenticity contributes to courage—the courage to be different. And the real test of courage comes when we're in the minority. Because we tend to be social animals, we often have difficulty standing alone in our opinions. As the playwright Henrik Ibsen said, "The strongest man in the world is he who stands most alone." Certainly we're all called to stand alone at times. When we're at our most authentic, following the dictates of our heart and mind and doing what we believe is right, we sometimes displease others whom we'd prefer to accommodate. And when what we believe so strongly turns out to be wrong, we're called to summon up the courage to acknowledge our error. Authenticity implies doing things we really believe in, activities that reverberate with our needs, values, and dreams—in short, activities that have meaning for us.

Searching for Meaning

The Spanish poet Pedro Calderon de la Barca once said, "Even in dreams doing good is not wasted." The pursuit of goodness leaves a pleasant aftertaste when we wake up in the morning, motivating us to continue in its path. Authentic people look for a sense of meaning in daily life. Just living, without finding meaning in what we're doing, results in an empty existence indeed. We need to transcend feelings of boredom, disconnection, and alienation—frequent visitors in this age of plenty and convenience. We accomplish that transcendence by forming an attachment to something larger than ourselves.

Authenticity and humankind's search for meaning are like twins. Only when our personal activities are consistent with our values, commitments, and other important elements of the concept of ourselves can meaning be attained. And only in the company of meaning can happiness be found. Actually, the Greek word that's usually translated as happiness—*eudaimonia* (literally "good spirit," as we saw earlier)—would more properly be translated as the feelings accompanying behavior consistent with one's true potential. The *daimon* in *eudaimonia*—"spirit"—is that which strives to create direction and meaning in our lives.

The educator Helen Keller once said, "Many persons have a wrong idea of what constitutes true happiness. It is not attained through self-gratification but through fidelity to a worthy purpose." She knew this better than most people, being both blind and deaf due to a severe illness at infancy. Through a heroic effort on her part and that of her teacher Anne Sullivan (who knew what blindness meant, having been partially cured of it), Keller learned to read and write in braille. As an adult she devoted her life to helping the deaf and the blind. Her many books became the basis for a play by William Gibson, *The Miracle Worker,* which won a Pulitzer Price and was later made into a motion picture. Helen Keller toured the world promoting the cause of people similarly afflicted. Her spirituality, selflessness, courage, and perseverance inspired many, as did her civility, compassion, and caring. Those traits served *her* well too, contributing to her self-worth and emotional health.

Most of us would like to be remembered as people who did their best to help others. In my own personal journey (through my work with organizational leaders), I seek meaning in helping others develop their full potential, acting as a guide in their inner journey and encouraging them to actualize their strengths and face their limitations. I want people to be aware of the fact that mental health is the result of *choice*. It's not a *given*. I want people to own their own lives, not to be puppets manipulated by others. I want to help people find a meaningful balance in their lives. My hope is that when people in leadership positions are committed to such goals, they'll positively affect the organizations they run. In a small way, then, I'm trying to contribute to the creation of organizations in which people find purpose, feel a sense of wholeness, perceive themselves as complete and alive, have the opportunity to learn and grow, and believe that they can make a difference. Sometimes I dare to hope that in an even smaller way (who knows?) the creation of such organizations—places that are fair to everyone, places that abhor injustice—will contribute to a better society.

I encourage executives to create what I call "authentizotic organizations." The goal of such organizations is reflected in the two Greek words, *authenteekos* and *zoteekos,* on which the label is based. The first conveys the idea that the organization is *authentic.* As a workplace label, *authenticity* implies that an organization has a compelling connective quality for its employees in its vision, mission, culture, and structure. In other words, it creates meaning for the people who work there. The second term, *zoteekos,* means "vital to life." In the organizational context, it describes the way in which people are invigorated by their work. It applies to organizations that allow for self-assertion in the workplace and produce a sense of effectiveness and competency, autonomy, initiative, creativity, entrepreneurship, and industry—organizations in which people feel generally happy.

While the search for meaning has to encompass the workplace, it can't be restricted to it. As I suggested earlier, it's my strong belief that our own happiness increases when we give happiness away—a practice more common away from one's desk. Of the people I interviewed who were actively involved in volunteer activities, all reported an increased feeling of well-being when undertaking their particular volunteer project; they felt energized and alive. They reported that engaging in such activities filled up an emptiness within—the latter being the price many pay for rampant individualism. When we reach out and help others, moving from individualistic to good-citizenship behavior, we tend to be happier.

Egotism is the anesthetic that dulls the pain of stupidity. It may be an effective tranquilizer, but it doesn't diminish the foolishness of hanging on to such a life strategy. Narcissists end up lonely, and unhappy to boot. Those people who are the most self-focused, who have the greatest difficulty reaching out to others, are the unhappiest.

Epictetus once said, "All human beings seek the happy life, but many confuse the means—for example, wealth and status—with that life itself. This misguided focus on the means to a good life makes people get further from the happy life. The really worthwhile things are the virtuous activities that make up the happy life, not the external means that may seem to produce it." Finding meaning through good works that go beyond rampant individualism brings people together, helping them to feel part of the human community and allowing them to feel good about themselves. Think about the people who work for the Red Cross or *Médecins sans frontières.* These people have a commitment to their work that's hard to match in other settings. They radiate a sense of responsibility, nurturance, and civility, believing that their contribution will make for a better world. Their work gives them a deep sense of satisfaction and happiness.

One of the people who have most extensively explored humankind's search for meaning is the father of logotherapy, Victor Frankl. During his time in a number of Nazi death camps he came to see that the survivors were the ones who were able to transcend suffering by finding meaning in life in spite of the horrific circumstances they found themselves in. He recognized that apathetic behavior was less common and the death rate lower among those concentration camp inmates who retained a purpose for living and dying.

Frankl made it his life work to advocate that humankind's primary motivational force is the search for meaning and purpose. He argued that people aren't really in pursuit of happiness; rather, they're looking for *reasons* to be happy. If they attempt to make the best of a given situation, to find meaning in even the grimmest circumstances, they will achieve satisfaction. Frankl also promoted "tragic optimism," which is the ability to turn suffering into human achievement, to strive for improvement no matter how bad things look, to be motivated (in spite of life's transitory nature) toward responsible action.

Without meaning, says Frankl, we end up in an existential vacuum; we suffer from "abyss-experiences" and simply give up. If we're to be mentally healthy, we need the feeling that there's a purpose to life and that what we're doing is consistent with our values, commitments, and other important aspects of self-identity. Thus a sense of directedness and intentionality, whatever form this may take, helps our mental equilibrium.

Meaning can be found all around us. It can be discovered in relationships, work, a good cause, and/or religious beliefs. What all of these meaning-sources share is a motivation to go beyond narrow self-interests, to engage in something on a more substantial scale. While selfish people, preoccupied with their own happiness, look out for number one, selfless people attempt to bring happiness to others—and therein lies their happiness. Since people engaged in altruistic behavior feel better about themselves and the world, altruistic behavior can be reframed—here's a paradox!—as acting in one's own self-interest.

Financier George Soros can be held up as an example of an individual who has gone a long way toward finding meaning through altruistic behavior. Soros was born in Budapest to a prosperous Jewish family, but his childhood was disrupted by the Nazis' entry into Hungary. To escape the concentration camps, the family had to leave the country. The uprooting of his family made quite an impression on young Soros, marking him for the rest of his life. The family moved to London, where Soros chose philosophy as his field of study. For practical reasons, he soon abandoned his plans to become a philosopher and instead joined a merchant bank. Over time he established his own investment fund, which became extremely successful (and remained so until recently he ran into some problems). Instead of looking out for number one and retaining all of his earnings for himself, he used a generous share of his profits to create a network of philanthropic organizations. Much of the work of the Soros Foundations has been directed at Eastern Europe—starting with Hungary—where he has awarded scholarships, provided technical assistance, and helped modernize schools and businesses. His way of finding meaning in life has been through building stable democracies in these countries.

Knowing Oneself

Authenticity and meaning aren't gifts; they're earned, the culmination of learning from many hardships. As the saying goes, "No mistakes, no experience; no experience, no wisdom." Wisdom is usually found only in people who've gone through difficult life experiences and surmounted the setbacks that those experiences presented. As the French novelist Marcel Proust noted, "We don't receive wisdom; we must discover it for ourselves after a journey that no one can take for us or spare us." Failure and anguish pave the royal road to insight. Mistakes are the usual bridge between inexperience and wisdom. Defeat is thus the cornerstone of wisdom, the complement to authenticity. And the memories that defeat leaves us are great catalysts for self-reflection.

There's a story about a famous Zen master who was approached by a young monk wanting to become his disciple. After the novice told him about his wishes, the Zen master invited him to have tea with him. When the tea was prepared, the master began pouring the tea in the novice's cup. Surprisingly, when the cup was full, the master didn't stop. He kept on pouring, letting the tea spill out. The novice asked him why he was he doing such a thing. The master replied, "Your mind is like the cup. It is bursting full. There is no place for anything new. I cannot teach you anything. Go away, and come back when you have made some room." Narcissism—being full of oneself—and self-knowledge rarely go together. To acquire self-knowledge, to acquire wisdom, we need an open mind; we need to be prepared to experience new things. As the book of Proverbs says, "Experience is the mother of wisdom."

Being authentic, creating meaning, and possessing wisdom are closely related human dynamics that reinforce and build on each other. They all focus on the existential journey that is our life. And if we want to understand what our life is all about, we have to face the facts about ourselves, unpleasant as these may be at times. Being prepared to look into ourselves is a necessary condition for acquiring wisdom.

As the Greek dramatist Aeschylus puts it, "Wisdom comes through suffering." Only by understanding the unpleasant parts of ourselves can we deflect and overcome our darker side. Wisdom comes not only come from experience but also from meditating on experience. On the gate of the temple of Apollo in Delphi were written the words "Know thyself"—words that still reverberate today.

Wisdom implies a high degree of personal and interpersonal functioning. The psychoanalyst and human development scholar Erik Erikson tied wisdom to integrity and generativity (the desire to care for others). He clarified the different challenges we face at each stage of the life cycle to reach increasingly higher level of functioning as life unfolds, identifying a whole host of traits essential to wisdom. In Erikson's schema, wisdom implies a concern for the well-being of others, an affirmation of differences, a tolerance for ambiguity, and an acceptance of the uncertainties that our world brings. I also think that it implies the capacity for empathy and mood regulation, the ability to listen and understand, and the capacity for judgment and advice. Finally, wisdom involves a degree of mastery over strategies concerning the conduct and meaning of life, a knowledge of life's obligations and goals, and a degree of understanding of the human condition. But in the end, as Epictetus reminds us, wisdom is revealed through action, not talk.

Acceptance of one's self and one's past life isn't always easy. All of us have a great capacity to delude ourselves, a unique defensive structure composed of many resistances that need to be overcome as we go through the process of personal discovery. Until we break down those resistances and understand ourselves, we're not really free, nor really alive. Understanding our inner world is the key to conquering our outer world—and to arriving at a state of wisdom. If we conquer ourselves, we conquer all. To be a good judge of people, we need to know what we ourselves are all about.

So how do we gain self-knowledge? In more religious periods of history, people spent much of their time in church. Prayer gave them an opportunity to reflect on life and take stock. Nowadays, however, structured religious activities are less common, though quiet moments with ourselves are just important today as they were in the past. We all need time for self-renewal and self-reflection. For reasons of personal development, we all need time alone with ourselves to examine what we're doing and think about what's right and good for us. We need time to contemplate our strengths and weaknesses. We need time to play with our imagination. We need time to dream.

Arriving at self-reflection alone isn't always possible. Paradoxically, in the search for meaningful quiet moments for self-reflection, we may need professional help. We may need to consult someone who will listen to our ideas and fantasies, help us make sense of our daydreams and night dreams, get us unstuck when we're caught in a vicious circle, help us see crucial linkages between past and present, and guide us into a better future. Dialogue of this sort isn't typically comfortable. Because it requires opening up to another person to an extent that we don't often experience, it demands tremendous trust. But finding a companion for our journey of self-discovery can pay great dividends in terms of achieving personal growth, seeing new alternatives, and preventing errors that would haunt us later in life.

Many people who lack the courage to engage on such a personal journey instead adopt what some psychologists describe as "the manic defense." They run away from self-discovery—and can't stop running. Suffering from "hurry sickness," they delude themselves into thinking that activity equals happiness. They're afraid that if they stop running, they'll see the emptiness of their lives. Though time is short, these people waste what years they have in pointless activity. What are they running for? What are they running to? As Mahatma Gandhi once said, "There is more to life than increasing its speed." For people who rely on the manic defense, most of life has been spent before they know what it is and means.

Unless we're willing to forego happiness, we need to strive for wisdom and refuse to become victims of hurry sickness. We don't want to become one of those unfortunates who discover that life is what happens while they're busy making other plans. We need to

reflect on what's important to us and make an effort to set our priorities accordingly. If we choose to do that which we really enjoy and live life to the fullest, we've got a serious shot at attaining happiness.

Smelling the Flowers

Finding happiness isn't like arriving at a station. We don't one day get to a certain place and feel flooded with happiness. No miracles happen when we arrive at a final destination. There *is* no final destination. There will always be a next stop. *Happiness is the way in which we travel.*

There's another Zen story about a person who had been told about an enchanted valley at a place far away, a valley that was full of the most beautiful flowers. She decided to search out this place and see it for herself. Though she set off eagerly, she was astounded at the length of the journey. Days turned into weeks, weeks into months, and months into years. Finally, totally exhausted, she arrived at the edge of a forest where she found an old man leaning against a tree. She said, "Old man, I have been traveling now for longer than I care to remember. I have been looking for an enchanted valley with beautiful flowers. Please, could you tell me how far I still have to go?" The response from the old man was, "The valley is right behind you. Didn't you notice? You passed it on the way."

As this parable illustrates, it's important that we focus more on the route, the scenery, and our fellow travelers than on the destination. We need to grasp happiness on the way, enjoying the journey rather than impatiently counting the kilometers. Too many people spend their lives climbing ladders only to find out that their ladders were placed against the wrong wall. We need to enjoy the little things, since they often turn out to be the big things in the end.

Socrates once said that an unexamined life isn't worth living. We could equally well say that an unlived life isn't worth examining. If we're serious about the pursuit of happiness, we have to make the journey worthwhile, cherishing each moment. To quote Marcus Aurelius, the philosopher-king, "It is not death that a man should fear, but he should fear never beginning to live." It's later than we think!

Suggested Reading

Even though I've avoided using references in the text, I've listed below a number of books and articles that were influential in my writing of this book.

Argyle, M. (1987). *The Psychology of Happiness*. London: Methuen.

Argyle, M. (1997). Is Happiness is Cause of Health? *Psychology and Health, 12, 769-781.*

Bowlby, J. (1969). *Attachment and Loss*. (Vol. 1: Attachment). New York: Basic Books.

Buss, D. M. (2000). The Evolution of Happiness. *American Psychologist*, 55(1), 15-23.

Cousins, N. (1991). *Anatomy of an Illness*. New York: W. W. Norton.

Csikszentmihalyi, M. (1990). *Flow: The Psychology of Optimal Experience*. New York: Harper and Row.

Diener, E., Eunkook, M. S., Lucas, R. E., & Smith, H. L. (1999). Subjective Well-Being: Three Decades of Progress. *Psychological Bulletin, 125*(2), 276-302.

Erikson, E. H. (1963). *Childhood and Society*. New York: W.W. Norton & Society.

Frankl, V. (1962). *Man's Search for Meaning: An Introduction to Logotherapy*. Boston: Beacon Press.

Friedman, M., & Ulmer, D. (1984). *Treating Type A Behavior-and Your Heart*. New York: Knopf.

Freud, S. (1929). Civilization and its Discontents. In J. Strachey (Ed.), *Standard Edition of the Complete Psychological Works of Sigmund Freud* (Vol. 21). London: Hogarth Press and the Institute of Psychoanalysis.

Kahneman, D., Diener, E., & Schwarz, N. (Eds.). (1999). *Well-Being: The Foundations of Hedonistic Psychology*. New York: Russell Sage Foundation.

Kets de Vries, M. F. R. (1995). *Life and Death in the Executive Fast Lane: Essays on Irrational Organizations and their Leaders*. San Francisco: Jossey-Bass.

Kets de Vries, M. F. R. (2001). *Struggling with the Demon: Perspectives in Individual and Organizational Irrationality*. Madison, Conn.: Psychosocial Press.

Lichtenberg, J. (1989). *Psychoanalysis and Motivation*. Hillsdale, NJ: Analytic Press.

Russell, B. (1930). *The Conquest of Happiness*. London: George Allen & Unwin.

Seligman, M. E. P. (1990). *Learned Optimism*. New York: Simon & Schuster.

Seligman, M. E. P., & Csikszentmihalyi, M. (2000). Positive Psychology: An Introduction. *American Psychologist, 55*(1), 5-14.

White, R. (1966). *Lives in Progress*. New York: Holt, Rinehart and Winston.

About the Author

Manfred Kets de Vries holds the Raoul de Vitry d'Avaucourt Chair of Human Resource Management at INSEAD, France. He is the Clinical Professor of Leadership Development. He received an economics degree from the University of Amsterdam and a MBA and DBA from the Harvard Business School. He is also practicing psychoanalyst/psychotherapist and a member of the Canadian Psychoanalytic Society and the International Psychoanalytic Association. He has held professorships at McGill University, the Ecole des Hautes Etudes Commerciales and the Harvard Business School. He has lectured at management institutions all over the world. Kets de Vries' research interests include leadership, career dynamics, executive stress, entrepreneurship, family business, succession planning, cross-cultural management, and the dynamics of corporate transformation and change. Kets de Vries is a member of a large number of editorial boards. He is program director of INSEAD's top management program "The Challenge of Leadership: Developing Your Emotional Intelligence" and co-program director of the Diploma/Master's degree program "Coaching and Consulting for Change." Kets de Vries has authored, co-authored and edited 48 books and written more than 400 articles and book chapters apart from a large number of case studies. His books include The Neurotic Organization (1990), Leaders, Fools and Impostors (1993), Life and Death in the Executive Fast Lane (1995), The Happiness Equation (2002), Are Leaders Made or Are They Born? The Case of Alexander the Great (2004), Leadership by Terror (2004), The New Russian Business Elite (2006), The Leadership Mystique (2006), The Leader on the Couch (2006), Coach and Couch (2007), Sex, Money, Happiness, and Death: The Quest for Authenticity (2009), Reflections on Leadership and Character (2009), Reflections on Leadership and Career (2010), The Coaching Kaleidoscope (2010), The Hedgehog Effect: The Secrets of High Performance Teams (2011) and Mindful Leadership Coaching: Journeys into the Interior (2014), You Will Meet a Tall Dark Stranger: Executive Coaching Challenges (2015) and Telling Fairy Tales in the Boardroom: How to Make Sure Your Organization Lives Happily Ever After (2015) and Riding the Leadership Roller Coaster: A Psychological Observer's Guide (2017).His books have been translated into fifteen languages. Six of his numerous case studies have received the best case of the year award. The Financial Times, Le Capital, Wirtschaftswoche, and The Economist have judged Manfred Kets de Vries one of Europe's leading management thinkers. Kets de Vries has conducted executive development seminars for a number of the of the most admired companies in Europe, the USA, Asia, the Middle East and Africa and serves as a consultant in organizational design/transformation and strategic human resource management at many of the top European and U.S. corporations. He was the first fly fisherman in Outer Mongolia and is a member of the Explorer's Club.

www.ingramcontent.com/pod-product-compliance
Lightning Source LLC
Chambersburg PA
CBHW041103110426
42740CB00043B/140